Make Money with AI

A STEP-BY-STEP GUIDE TO BUILDING WEALTH USING ARTIFICIAL INTELLIGENCE

CAMILO QUINONES GARCIA

Contents

Introduction

In 2023, a small online business owner named Sarah decided to try something new. She started using an AI tool to handle customer inquiries. Within a month, her revenue doubled. The AI worked tirelessly, answering questions and solving problems faster than any human could. Sarah's story is not an isolated incident. Across the globe, entrepreneurs are discovering the power of AI to transform their businesses and, in turn, their lives.

This book is built on a simple yet powerful idea: AI can unlock profitable opportunities for entrepreneurs. Whether launching a startup or scaling an existing business, AI can be a game-changer. It offers strategies to build wealth in ways that were not possible before. The goal is to guide you through this landscape, offering insights and tools you can apply immediately.

This book is a go-to resource that you'll want to share with your family, friends, and colleagues. It's designed to be more than just a guide—a conversation starter. It combines practical insights with real-world examples, providing the tools you need to succeed in this digital age. You'll find stories and strategies that are easy to understand and apply, regardless of your technical background.

The structure of this book follows a logical progression. We'll start with the basics of AI, demystifying what it is and what it can do. Next, we'll explore how AI impacts various industries, from retail to real estate. Then, we'll dive into key strategies for integrating AI into your business. Each chapter builds on the last, leading you toward a comprehensive understanding of AI's potential to create wealth.

This book is crafted for adult entrepreneurs eager to leverage AI for financial success. You might be a seasoned business owner or someone just starting. Either way, you'll find valuable insights explicitly tailored for you. The content is designed to meet you where you are, with practical advice and actionable strategies that apply directly to your business context.

Many entrepreneurs share common motivations and face similar challenges when exploring AI. You're likely driven to innovate and stay competitive, but you may wonder where to start. You might need to pay more attention to the cost of AI or the skills required to implement it. This book addresses these concerns head-on, offering solutions to help you overcome each hurdle.

The value of this book lies in its practicality. It's not just about theory or abstract ideas. You'll find actionable strategies and real-world examples demonstrating how AI can enhance your business. We'll explore case studies and success stories that illustrate AI's transformative potential, giving you a clear roadmap to follow.

Among the unique selling points of this book are the industry-specific insights and a curated AI toolkit. These are designed to give you a competitive edge, offering resources and strategies tailored to your field. Whether you work in healthcare, finance, or any other sector, you'll find tools and tips that apply directly to your needs.

As we progress, you can expect to gain a deeper understanding of AI and its impact on wealth creation. By the end of this book, you'll know how to use AI to enhance your competitive edge, improve efficiency, and, ultimately, build wealth. You'll be equipped with the knowledge and skills to navigate the AI landscape, transforming challenges into opportunities confidently.

I invite you to dive in, explore the possibilities, and embrace the future of entrepreneurship with AI. Together, we'lldiscover how this powerful tool can redefine what it means to succeed in today's digital economy.

CHAPTER 1

Understanding AI and Its Financial Potential

In the bustling city of Shenzhen, a small electronics shop owner named Liu was overwhelmed with the daily grind. Inventory checks, customer queries, and financial balancing were consuming his time. A friend suggested he explore AI solutions. Skeptical but curious, Liu implemented an AI system to manage his inventory and respond to frequent customer inquiries. To his astonishment, the AI streamlined operations, and sales surged by over 30% within just a few months. Stories like Liu's are becoming increasingly common, highlighting AI's potential to simplify tasks and significantly boost profitability. As entrepreneurs navigate the complexities of today's market, AI stands out as a beacon of opportunity, promising to revolutionize how businesses operate.

1.1 DEMYSTIFYING AI: WHAT EVERY ENTREPRENEUR NEEDS TO KNOW

Artificial Intelligence, often referred to as AI, is a term that can seem daunting at first. However, at its core, it's a system of algorithms and data designed to perform tasks that typically require human Intelligence. These tasks range from recognizing speech to making decisions or even driving a car. Machine learning is a pivotal component of AI, where systems learn from data and improve over time. Think of it as a computer learning to recognize patterns, much like a child learning to differentiate between shapes and colors. Natural language processing, another crucial aspect, allows machines to understand and respond to human language. This technology is behind chatbots and virtual assistants that can answer questions or provide recommendations. Robotics and automation are extensions of AI, where machines perform tasks with precision and efficiency, often outperforming human capabilities in speed and accuracy.

The evolution of AI has been marked by significant milestones. One of the most notable was IBM's Deep Blue defeating world chess champion Garry Kasparov in 1997, a testament to AI's burgeoning capabilities. Fast forward to 2016, and Google's AlphaGo achieved a similar feat by besting a human champion in the complex game of Go. These events captured the world's imagination, demonstrating AI's potential to handle intricate tasks. Yet, the journey didn't stop there. Today, AI is more accessible than ever, with applications that can benefit businesses of all sizes. The advancements in AI have democratized technology, allowing even small companies to leverage their power without requiring vast resources or technical expertise.

Current AI capabilities are nothing short of remarkable. Virtual assistants like Siri and Alexa have become household names, offering convenience at our fingertips. These AI-powered tools can manage schedules, control smart home devices, and even provide weather updates. In business, predictive analytics powered by AI is revolutionizing marketing by analyzing consumer data to forecast trends and tailor campaigns. This ability to anticipate customer needs leads to better-targeted marketing efforts and increased sales. However, despite its impressive capabilities, AI has its limitations. It excels in processing vast amounts of data and performing specific tasks but needs more intrinsic creativity and emotional understanding. Human oversight remains crucial, especially when ethical decisions arise, ensuring AI complements rather than replaces human intuition and judgment.

As you explore the potential of AI, it's essential to acknowledge these limitations. While AI can automate numerous tasks, it cannot replicate the nuanced creativity and emotional Intelligence that humans provide. Decision-making in AI relies on data and established algorithms, which means it can struggle with scenarios requiring ethical considerations or empathy. Therefore, a symbiotic relationship between humans and AI is vital, where machines handle repetitive tasks, freeing humans to focus on strategic and creative endeavors. This collaboration can lead to innovative solutions and drive businesses forward, ensuring that AI is a tool for enhancement rather than replacement.

1.2 AI IN BUSINESS: TRANSFORMATIVE POWER AND PROFITABILITY

AI has rapidly become a cornerstone for transforming various business functions, offering tools that redefine how companies operate and engage with their customers. Take customer service, for example. Businesses have adopted chatbots to provide round-the-clock assistance, efficiently managing inquiries and resolving issues. These AI-driven chatbots reduce wait times significantly and improve customer satisfaction by providing immediate responses. In marketing, AI's role is equally transformative. It enables personalized marketing campaigns that target consumers based on their preferences and behavior. This precision ensures that marketing efforts are not just shots in the dark but are thoughtfully tailored, increasing engagement and conversion rates. Meanwhile, AI optimizes supply chain processes in operations, forecasting demand with accuracy that reduces inventory costs and minimizes waste. This streamlining ensures businesses remain agile and responsive, a critical advantage in today's fast-paced market.

The profitability enhancements from AI adoption are substantial. By automating routine tasks, businesses cut down on labor costs and reallocate resources to more strategic areas. This automation translates to immediate cost savings and operational efficiencies that drive profitability. Furthermore, AI enhances the customer experience by providing seamless interactions and personalized services, fostering loyalty and repeat business. Companies find that the initial investment in AI tools often yields a significant return through increased sales and customer retention. Businesses across industries report cost reductions and revenue growth, underscoring AI's capability to significantly boost the bottom line.

AI's versatility is evident across various sectors, showcasing its adaptability in meeting diverse business needs. In healthcare, AI assists in diagnostics by analyzing medical images precisely, supporting doctors in making faster, more accurate diagnoses. This application enhances patient outcomes and optimizes resource allocation within medical facilities. In the financial sector, AI plays a pivotal role in fraud detection, analyzing transaction patterns to flag suspicious activities. This proactive approach protects assets and builds trust with consumers. Agriculture, too, benefits from AI through yield optimization technologies that analyze soil conditions and weather patterns, guiding farmers to maximize their harvests sustainably. These examples illustrate AI's potential to revolutionize industry practices, driving efficiency and innovation.

Real-world case studies provide concrete evidence of AI's impact on business success. Netflix, for instance, uses AI algorithms to power its recommendation engine, offering personalized content suggestions that keep viewers engaged and subscribed. This tailored approach has been vital to Netflix's ability to dominate the streaming market. Similarly, Amazon leverages AI in its logistics operations, optimizing delivery routes and inventory management to ensure timely deliveries and reduce costs. These AI-driven strategies enhance customer satisfaction and contribute significantly to the companies'competitive advantage and profitability. Such examples illustrate the profound benefits of integrating AI into business models, offering lessons that other businesses can learn from and apply.

Case Study: AI in Action

One standout example of AI's transformative power can be seen in the retail giant Amazon. By employing advanced AI algorithms, Amazon optimizes its logistics and inventory management to ensure products efficiently reach customers. The AI systems analyze traffic patterns, weather conditions, and historical delivery data to determine the most efficient routes and warehousing strategies. This not only minimizes delivery times but also reduces logistical costs significantly. The result is a streamlined operation that keeps customers satisfied and loyal. Amazon's approach highlights the potential for AI to revolutionize logistics, setting a benchmark for businesses seeking to improve operational efficiency through technology.

1.3 THE ECONOMICS OF AI: COST-EFFECTIVE SOLUTIONS FOR ENTREPRENEURS

When considering the adoption of artificial Intelligence, it's natural to focus on the economics. The initial costs of integrating AI into a business can seem daunting. There's the hardware, software, and sometimes the need to hire experts to get things rolling. However, these upfront expenses must be weighed against the long-term savings and revenue growth AI can bring. Once implemented, AI can automate routine tasks, analyze data in real time, and predict trends that would otherwise require extensive human resources. Over time, these efficiencies can lead to significant cost reductions. For example, according to a McKinsey report, businesses report cutting operational costs by 10 to 19% thanks to AI. This demonstrates that while the initial investment might feel substantial, the return on investment often justifies the expenditure, leading to enhanced profitability and sustained growth.

The good news for small to medium enterprises is that many cost-effective AI tools and platforms are now available. Open-source platforms like TensorFlow and Keras provide robust frameworks for developing AI applications without hefty licensing fees. These platforms, backed by a community of developers, offer flexibility and scalability. Additionally, cloud-based AI solutions such as Amazon Web Services (AWS) and Google Cloud AI provide scalable computing power on a pay-as-you-go basis, enabling businesses to expand or reduce their AI capabilities as needed without investing in expensive infrastructure. These solutions are particularly beneficial for companies looking to experiment with AI, as they offer the flexibility to scale up or down based on project requirements and budget constraints. This accessibility ensures that even smaller enterprises can leverage AI's advantages without breaking the bank.

The scalability and flexibility of AI solutions make them particularly attractive for growing businesses. Cloud-based AI services allow companies to adjust their computing power according to their needs. This flexibility is crucial for companies experiencing rapid growth or seasonal fluctuations, as they can increase capacity during peak times and scale back when demand decreases. Moreover, modular AI systems, which enable businesses to add or remove functionalities as required, offer another layer of adaptability. Companies can start small, focusing on a specific area, such as customer service or marketing. They can gradually expand their AI capabilities across different functions as they gain confidence and see results. This approach mitigates risk and ensures that AI investments align with the company's strategic goals and growth trajectory.

The potential return on investment from AI is difficult to ignore. AI can drive significant revenue growth by automating tasks and improving operational efficiency. For example, enterprises that have adopted AI report revenue increases of up to 10% or more. This is achieved by optimizing processes, enhancing customer experience, and reducing costs. AI'sability to predict consumer behavior and tailor marketing efforts can increase sales and customer retention, further boosting ROI. Moreover, AI's predictive capabilities allow businesses to make informed decisions, reducing the risk of costly errors. These benefits underscore AI's economic viability, making it a compelling option for companies looking to improve their bottom line.

Interactive Element: AI ROI Calculator

Consider using an AI ROI calculator to get a clearer picture of the potential financial benefits AI could bring to your business. Input your current operational costs, expected savings, and possible revenue growth into the calculator to see projected ROI over time. This tool can help you decide when and where to implement AI in your operations.

With real-world examples showcasing AI's financial impact, it's clear that the technology can be a valuable asset for businesses seeking to stay competitive. Companies like Tesla and Airbnb have successfully integrated AI to streamline operations and enhance customer engagement, resulting in significant cost savings and revenue growth. These examples highlight how strategic AI adoption can lead to substantial financial benefits, reinforcing that AI is not just a technological trend but a viable economic strategy for businesses of all sizes.

1.4 AI MYTHS DEBUNKED: SEPARATING HYPE FROM REALITY

A bustling coffee shop in Portland, Oregon, owner Jake believed AI was reserved for the tech giants of Silicon Valley. He thought integrating AI into his business would require resources and technical know-how far beyond his reach. This misconception is widespread. Many believe AI is only for Google or Amazon, dismissing its potential for their ventures. The myth that AI is exclusively for large corporations has long been a barrier for small businesses. However, AI has become increasingly accessible. Tools like Jasper, an AI writing assistant, and Dialpad Ai, a customer intelligence platform, have been designed with smaller enterprises in mind, offering affordability and ease of use. These tools demonstrate that AI is not the exclusive playground of tech behemoths. Instead, it's a versatile resource that can benefit businesses of all sizes by streamlining operations and enhancing customer interactions.

Entrepreneurs should recognize this shift and explore how AI can meet their specific needs without overwhelming complexity.

The complexity of AI often intimidates business owners. The intricate algorithms and vast data sets can seem impossible. Yet, today's AI tools are crafted to simplify these complexities. Entry-level applications, like Seventh Sense for optimizing email marketing or Speechify for text-to-speech functionalities, provide a straightforward introduction to AI'scapabilities. These tools don't demand a background in computer science. Instead, they enable entrepreneurs to enhance their operations with minimal training. This shift toward user-friendly AI means business owners can focus on strategic growth rather than getting bogged down in technical details. The practical nature of these tools also allows for gradual integration, letting businesses scale their AI usage as they become more comfortable with the technology. This accessibility ensures that AI is no longer a daunting prospect but a practical tool for enhancing business efficiency and innovation.

Furthermore, the fear that AI will replace human jobs is a nuanced topic. While AI can automate repetitive tasks, it is not a substitute for human creativity or empathy. In fact, AI often requires human oversight to function optimally. Collaborative tools like AI Agent Assist, which supports customer service agents in real time, showcase the symbiotic relationship between humans and machines. AI handles data processing and pattern recognition, while humans provide the judgment and strategic thinking that machines cannot replicate. This collaboration enhances productivity and allows employees to focus on tasks that require a human touch. Rather than viewing AI as a competitor, businesses should embrace it as a partner that can free up time and resources for more meaningful work. By leveraging AI in this way, companies can foster a more engaged and innovative workforce.

Supporting these ideas with evidence, a study by McKinsey highlights that nearly half of the businesses using AI have seen significant improvements in their operations and cost savings. Experts in the field emphasize that AI's role is to augment human capabilities, not replace them. This perspective is echoed in industry reports highlighting the growing trend of human-AI collaboration across sectors. As AI becomes more integrated into business practices, the focus shifts from fear of replacement to empowerment through enhanced capabilities. This approach allows businesses to capitalize on AI's strengths while maintaining the human elements that drive innovation and customer satisfaction.

In conclusion, separating the myths from reality reveals AI'strue potential for businesses of all sizes. When used correctly, it's a tool that can transform operations, enhance customer experiences, and drive profitability. By debunking these common misconceptions, entrepreneurs can approach AI with a fresh perspective, seeing it as an ally rather than an obstacle. This understanding paves the way for strategic integration, fostering a business environment where AI and human ingenuity work hand in hand. As we move forward, embracing AI's possibilities can lead to unprecedented growth and innovation, ensuring businesses remain competitive in an ever-evolving market.

CHAPTER 2

Laying the Groundwork for AI Integration

I magine a bustling bakery in the heart of Seattle, where the owner, Mark, juggled everything from baking to bookkeeping. With the demand for his artisanal bread rising, Mark was at a crossroads: either continue being overwhelmed or find an intelligent solution to streamline operations and grow his business. Enter AI. With the right tools, Mark could manage inventory, predict peak baking times, and even personalize customer interactions without needing an IT department. This transformative experience isn't just a tale of modern entrepreneurship; it's a blueprint for how artificial intelligence can revolutionize small businesses, empowering entrepreneurs like you to achieve more with less.

2.1 ASSESSING YOUR BUSINESS NEEDS: PREPARING FOR AI INTEGRATION

Conduct a thorough needs assessment before diving into AI integration to identify how AI can address specific business challenges and objectives. This begins with a SWOT analysis, a strategic planning technique to help businesses identify strengths, weaknesses, opportunities, and threats related to business competition or project planning. By understanding these elements, you can pinpoint areas where AI can benefit most. For instance, if customer service lags behind competitors, AI-driven chatbots might be a game-changer. Similarly, if inventory management is a pain point, predictive analytics could streamline stock levels, reducing waste and enhancing efficiency. This systematic approach ensures that AI solutions address your unique challenges without unnecessary complexity.

Aligning AI goals with your broader business objectives is crucial for successful integration. Establish clear AI objectives that complement your strategic goals, ensuring that every AI initiative supports your company's overall mission. For instance, if your business aims to enhance customer satisfaction, AI can analyze customer feedback to provide actionable insights. Strategic goal alignment workshops can foster this connection, bringing together stakeholders to discuss how AI can drive the business forward. Such workshops provide:

- A platform for discussing potential AI applications.
- Aligning them with company goals.
- Setting realistic expectations for outcomes.

This alignment maximizes AI's impact and ensures that all team members are on the same page and working towards common objectives.

Once you've established your AI goals, prioritize opportunities based on their potential impact and feasibility. Use an effect vs. feasibility matrix to evaluate different AI initiatives. This tool helps you weigh the benefits of an AI project against its complexity and resource requirements, enabling you to focus on high-impact, efficiently implementable solutions first. For example, automating email responses might be a quick win, improving customer satisfaction with minimal investment. On the other hand, developing a custom AI system for product recommendations might require more resources and time but could yield substantial long-term benefits. By prioritizing this, you can ensure that your AI efforts deliver tangible results without overextending your resources.

Engaging stakeholders early in the AI integration process is another critical step. From the outset, involve key team members and decision-makers to secure their buy-in and support. This can be achieved through stakeholder engagement strategies such as regular updates, collaborative planning sessions, and demonstrating the potential ROI of AI initiatives. Building cross-functional AI teams can also promote a culture of collaboration and innovation, as team members from different departments bring diverse perspectives and expertise. This diversity can lead to more creative solutions and a smoother implementation process, as all parties are invested in the initiative's success. Early engagement fosters a sense of ownership among stakeholders and helps identify potential roadblocks before they become significant issues.

Interactive Element: SWOT Analysis Worksheet

To start, consider completing a SWOT analysis worksheet specific to AI integration. List your business's strengths, weaknesses, opportunities, and threats related to AI. This exercise can help clarify where AI can make the most significant impact. Additionally, it can guide discussions with your team, ensuring that everyone understands how AI fits into the broader business strategy. Consider revisiting this worksheet periodically as your business and technology landscape evolves, allowing for continuous alignment and adaptation.

2.2 BUILDING A DATA-DRIVEN CULTURE: THE BACKBONE OF AI SUCCESS

Imagine a thriving small business in the heart of Chicago, bustling with activity yet struggling to make sense of the vast amounts of data flowing through it daily. This scenario illustrates where many entrepreneurs find themselves—aware of data's potential but unsure how to wield it effectively. Cultivating a data-first mindset can transform this challenge into an opportunity. It begins with fostering data literacy across your organization. This means investing in programs that teach employees how to interpret data, use it in decision-making, and understand its value. When your team sees data not just as numbers on a spreadsheet but as insights waiting to be uncovered, they become empowered to make smarter decisions. Leadership plays a crucial role here, setting the tone with a commitment to data-driven choices. By modeling this behavior, leaders inspire their teams to follow suit, embedding data-centric thinking into the company's fabric.

Establishing robust data governance practices is vital to ensure the quality and security of your data. Think of data governance as the framework that underpins your entire data strategy. It involves setting standards for data management, defining roles and responsibilities, and ensuring compliance with relevant regulations. By implementing a solid data governance framework, businesses can safeguard their data assets, ensuring they are accurate, consistent, and secure. This includes processes for data quality assurance, which involve regular checks to identify and rectify errors, providing the data you rely on is trustworthy. Effective data governance also means being proactive about security measures and protecting sensitive information from breaches. These practices protect your business and build trust with customers, who expect their data to be handled responsibly.

Investing in data infrastructure is another critical step in building a data-driven culture. This involves acquiring the necessary tools and technologies to efficiently store, process, and analyze data. Cloud-based data solutions offer an attractive option for many entrepreneurs, providing scalable storage and computing power without significant upfront investment. These solutions allow businesses to access and analyze data from anywhere, facilitating real-time decision-making. Real-time data analytics platforms further enhance your ability to make informed choices quickly, providing insights into customer behavior, market trends, and operational efficiency. Proper infrastructure investment allows your business to leverage data effectively, gaining a competitive edge in an increasingly data-driven world.

Continuous learning and education are essential for your workforce to handle data-centric tasks. Encourage a learning culture by offering workshops and training sessions focusing on data skills. These sessions should cover both the technical aspects, such as using data analytics tools, and the strategic ones, like interpreting data trends. Certification programs in data analytics can also provide employees with the credentials they need to excel in their roles, boosting confidence and competence. Staying updated with the latest data practices and tools is crucial in a rapidly evolving technological landscape. By promoting continuous learning, you ensure your team remains agile and equipped to meet the challenges of a data-driven future.

Reflection Section: Data-Driven Decision-Making

Take a moment to reflect on how data is currently used in your decision-making processes. Consider the following questions: How often do you consult data before making a significant business decision? Are there areas where data could play a more critical role? What steps can you take to increase data literacy within your organization? Use this reflection to identify areas for improvement and develop a plan for fostering a more data-driven culture. Remember, the goal is to make data an integral part of your business strategy, not just an afterthought.

2.3 CHOOSING THE RIGHT AI SOLUTIONS: TAILORING TECHNOLOGY TO YOUR INDUSTRY

Navigating the landscape of AI solutions can feel like exploring a vast library full of endless possibilities. It's crucial to approach this with a keen sense of purpose, ensuring the technology aligns with your industry needs. Begin with market research, which acts as your compass. Dive into industry trend analysis to uncover how AI transforms sectors like yours. For instance, in the retail industry, AI is reshaping everything from personalized customer experiences to inventory management.

Similarly, AI is making strides in diagnostics and patient care in healthcare. Understanding these trends provides a foundation for evaluating how AI can best serve your unique business goals. Additionally, examining competitor AI usage offers insights into your rivals' tools and strategies. This helps benchmark your efforts and inspires innovative applications that set your business apart. By keeping a pulse on industry advancements, you can identify AI solutions that are not just relevant but revolutionary for your operations.

Once you've gauged the landscape, the next step is critically evaluating vendor offerings. Not all AI solutions are created equal; selecting the right partner is crucial. Establish clear vendor comparison criteria that assess functionality, ease of integration, cost, and support services. Consider conducting pilot tests with a few select vendors. This approach lets you experience firsthand how their solutions perform within your business environment and whether they meet your expectations. During pilot testing, consider the vendor's responsiveness and willingness to customize solutions to fit your needs. These trials can reveal potential pitfalls and successes, guiding your final decision. Choosing a vendor that provides robust technology and aligns with your business ethos and future goals is essential. This strategic selection ensures a partnership that supports your long-term AI strategy.

In today's fast-evolving market, scalability and integration are non-negotiable. AI solutions must be able to grow alongside your business, adapting to increased demands and expanding functionalities. Consider scalability assessments to ensure the technology can handle growth without losing performance. API integration capabilities are equally important, as they determine how seamlessly the AI solution can connect with your existing systems. Whether it's integrating with your CRM, ERP, or other business platforms, the goal is to create a cohesive ecosystem where data flows smoothly and efficiently. This connectivity enhances operational efficiency and maximizes the utility of your existing technology investments. By prioritizing scalability and integration, you lay the groundwork for an AI infrastructure that evolves with your business, ensuring sustained value and adaptability.

User experience is often the unsung hero in successful AI deployment. Even the most advanced AI solution can only succeed if it is user-friendly. When evaluating potential AI tools, focus on user interface reviews to understand how intuitive and accessible the technology is for your team. A streamlined interface reduces the learning curve, enabling quicker adoption and more effective use. Gather feedback from pilot users within your organization, as their insights can provide valuable perspectives on usability and potential challenges. This feedback loop helps refine the selection process, ensuring that the chosen solution meets the needs of those who use it daily. Prioritizing user experience ensures your team can leverage AI to its full potential, driving productivity and innovation across the board.

2.4 OVERCOMING TECHNICAL BARRIERS: PRACTICAL TIPS FOR NON-TECH ENTREPRENEURS

In the vibrant world of entrepreneurship, technical barriers should be removed from your way. Many non-tech entrepreneurs often feel overwhelmed by the thought of incorporating AI into their businesses, fearing the complexities involved. However, these barriers can be effectively navigated with the right strategies. One of the most efficient ways to bridge the technical gap is by leveraging external expertise. Hiring AI consultants can bring a wealth of knowledge and experience to your project, helping you identify the most suitable AI applications for your needs. These experts can guide you through the intricacies of AI deployment, ensuring you make informed decisions tailored to your business objectives. Additionally, forming strategic partnerships with tech firms can provide ongoing support, offering insights into industry trends and access to cutting-edge technology. Such collaborations can prove invaluable, offering you the resources and expertise to implement AI solutions effectively.

Another key strategy in overcoming technical challenges is investing in user-friendly tools that simplify the AI deployment process. The rise of no-code AI platforms has made it easier than ever for businesses to integrate AI without the need for extensive technical knowledge. These platforms, such as Akkio and others, offer intuitive interfaces that allow you to build and deploy AI models with just a few clicks. Drag-and-drop AI solutions further reduce the complexity, enabling you to experiment with different applications without the need for programming skills. By choosing tools designed for ease of use, you empower your team to embrace AI confidently, making the technology more accessible and less intimidating. This approach streamlines the integration process and encourages a culture of innovation, as employees feel more comfortable experimenting with new ideas.

Training and support are crucial components in ensuring the successful integration of AI into your business. Providing comprehensive onboarding programs for AI tools can help your team get up to speed quickly, minimizing disruptions to your operations. These programs should be tailored to the specific needs of your business, focusing on the practical applications of AI relevant to your industry. Continuous technical support channels are equally important, offering your team a safety net as they navigate the learning curve. Access to expert advice and troubleshooting ensures issues are resolved swiftly, maintaining momentum and confidence in the AI initiatives. By prioritizing training and support, you foster an environment where employees are encouraged to develop their skills, leading to more excellent proficiency and enthusiasm for AI-driven projects.

Adopting a phased approach to AI integration can be a game-changer for non-tech entrepreneurs. By implementing AI in stages, you can manage complexity and reduce risks associated with large-scale deployments. Start with pilot projects that have clear objectives and measurable outcomes. These small-scale initiatives allow you to test the waters, assess the effectiveness of AI applications, and make necessary adjustments before a full-scale rollout. Incremental implementation strategies enable you to build on successes and learn from challenges, refining your approach. This systematic process mitigates risk and allows you to allocate resources more effectively, ensuring that AI integration aligns with your long-term business goals. Breaking down the integration process into manageable steps sets the stage for sustainable growth and innovation.

As we conclude this chapter, remember that overcoming technical barriers is not just about tackling challenges but about embracing opportunities for growth and innovation. By utilizing external expertise, investing in user-friendly tools, and fostering a culture of continuous learning, you empower your business to thrive in an AI-driven world. The journey may seem daunting initially, but with a strategic approach, you can transform potential obstacles into stepping stones toward success. By taking these steps, you're preparing your business for the future and setting a foundation for sustainable success in an ever-evolving digital landscape. As we progress, remember these strategies to ensure a smooth transition into AI, where possibilities are endless and innovation knows no bounds.

CHAPTER 3

Practical AI Application in Business

P icture a bustling call center where agents race against time to address a flood of customer inquiries. Every missed call or delayed response risks losing a customer. Enter AI: a game-changer poised to revolutionize customer service. Imagine AI chatbots tirelessly working around the clock, ensuring no customer query goes unanswered. These chatbots leverage natural language processing to understand customer queries and provide relevant responses instantaneously. Integrating these bots with your CRM systems allows you to offer personalized interactions that reflect the customer's history with your brand. This seamless integration means every customer feels valued and understood without human intervention at every touchpoint.

AI's ability to personalize customer interactions extends beyond chatbots. Picture AI-driven recommendation engines that anticipate what your customers want before they even know it themselves. These systems analyze past purchase behavior and preferences to suggest products or services, enhancing the shopping experience. Moreover, sentiment analysis tools can gauge customer emotions in real time, offering insights into how customers feel about your service or products. Understanding these sentiments allows you to tailor your responses and strategies to meet their needs, enhancing satisfaction and loyalty. Personalized interactions make customers feel special and drive engagement and conversions, creating a win-win scenario for both parties.

The power of AI to automate routine tasks in customer service is transformative. Consider the mundane yet essential tasks like ticket classification and FAQ response. AI can handle these efficiently, freeing human agents to tackle more complex issues requiring empathy and nuanced understanding. Automated ticket classification ensures that queries are directed to the correct department swiftly, reducing response times and enhancing efficiency. Similarly, AI can automate FAQ responses, instantly providing customers with accurate information. This automation reduces the workload on your team, allowing them to focus on building meaningful relationships with customers rather than getting bogged down by repetitive tasks.

AI analytics provide a strategic edge by offering insights into performance metrics that matter. Real-time performance dashboards can track key indicators such as response times, customer satisfaction scores, and issue resolution rates. These dashboards offer a comprehensive view of your customer service operations, enabling you to identify areas for improvement and celebrate successes. Moreover, predictive insights can inform staffing needs, ensuring you have the correct number of agents available to meet demand fluctuations. By leveraging these analytics, you can make informed decisions that enhance service quality and efficiency, positioning your business for success.

Case Study: Transforming Customer Service with AI

Consider the case of a mid-sized e-commerce company that implemented AI chatbots to handle customer inquiries. Initially overwhelmed by high call volumes, the company sought an innovative solution. By integrating AI chatbots equipped with natural language processing, they reduced wait times by 50% and increased customer satisfaction scores significantly. The chatbots seamlessly handled routine inquiries, allowing human agents to focus on complex issues. Real-time performance dashboards provided insights into peak call times, enabling better resource allocation. This strategic use of AI improved service and reduced operational costs by 30%, demonstrating the tangible benefits of AI in customer service.

As you explore AI's potential in customer service, consider how these tools can fit into your business model. AI offers not just a way to reduce costs but a means to elevate the entire customer experience. By implementing AI strategically, you can create a service environment that is both efficient and personalized, setting your business apart in a competitive marketplace.

3.1 OPTIMIZING OPERATIONS: AI-DRIVEN EFFICIENCY IMPROVEMENTS

AI emerges as a formidable ally in supply chain management, driving efficiency and precision like never before. Picture a bustling warehouse where every item is meticulously tracked and managed in real time. AI's predictive demand forecasting enables businesses to accurately anticipate market trends and consumer needs. By analyzing historical data and current market conditions, AI systems can predict demand fluctuations, ensuring that inventory levels are optimized to meet these demands without overstocking or shortages. This precision reduces carrying costs and minimizes waste, ultimately enhancing the bottom line. Inventory management, traditionally labor-intensive, becomes a streamlined operation with AI's intervention. Automated systems track inventory levels, reorder products, and even suggest optimal stock quantities, allowing businesses to maintain perfect balance effortlessly. This level of automation frees up valuable time and resources, enabling teams to focus on strategic initiatives.

In manufacturing, AI's impact is equally transformative, redefining production processes to increase efficiency and minimize waste. AI-driven quality control systems are adept at identifying defects and inconsistencies in real time, ensuring that only the highest quality products reach consumers. These systems use advanced image recognition and machine learning algorithms to detect even the slightest anomalies, significantly reducing the risk of defective products making it to market. Predictive maintenance, another AI innovation, revolutionizes machinery upkeep. By continuously monitoring equipment health and performance, AI systems can predict when maintenance is needed, preventing unexpected breakdowns and costly downtime. This proactive approach extends the lifespan of machinery and optimizes production schedules, ensuring that operations run smoothly and efficiently.

Logistics and distribution, critical components of any business operation, benefit immensely from AI's capabilities. AI powers route optimization algorithms, which analyze traffic patterns, weather conditions, and delivery schedules to determine the most efficient routes for transportation. This optimization reduces fuel consumption and delivery times, resulting in cost savings and improved service reliability. Dynamic fleet management, facilitated by AI, allows companies to adapt to changing conditions in real time. Whether rerouting vehicles to avoid congestion or reallocating resources during peak periods, AI provides insights that will enable quick decisions. These enhancements improve operational efficiency and elevate customer satisfaction by ensuring timely and reliable deliveries.

Workforce management is another area where AI proves invaluable, offering tools that optimize scheduling and productivity tracking. AI-driven shift scheduling algorithms consider employee availability, skill sets, and workload demands to create optimal schedules that maximize productivity and employee satisfaction. This intelligent scheduling reduces human error and ensures the right resources are in place at the right time. Employee performance analytics, powered by AI, offer insights into individual and team productivity, identifying areas for improvement and recognizing top performers. Businesses can implement targeted training programs and incentives that drive performance and engagement by understanding these dynamics. AI's contribution to workforce management streamlines operations and fosters a motivated, high-performing team.

3.2 MARKETING WITH AI: PERSONALIZATION AND PREDICTIVE ANALYTICS

In the bustling marketing realm, AI is a powerful tool transforming how businesses connect with customers. Imagine predicting what your customers want before they even realize it themselves. This is the promise of predictive analytics. By leveraging sophisticated algorithms, AI can analyze mountains of data to forecast customer behavior and preferences. It allows you to create customer segmentation models that break down your audience into distinct groups based on shared characteristics. This segmentation means you can tailor your marketing efforts to meet the specific needs of each group, enhancing the relevance of your campaigns.

Moreover, churn prediction algorithms can identify customers at risk of leaving, enabling you to take proactive steps to retain them. This foresight helps maintain customer loyalty and reduces turnover, ultimately boosting your bottom line. AI's predictive capabilities make your marketing strategies more targeted, precise, and effective.

Personalization is no longer just a buzzword; it's an expectation. AI empowers marketers to tailor messages to individual customers, enhancing engagement and satisfaction. Picture personalized email marketing campaigns that address recipients by name and offer products based on their previous interactions with your brand. This level of customization makes customers feel valued and understood, fostering stronger relationships. Furthermore, AI enables dynamic website content generation, adapting the content users see based on their behavior and preferences. Whether showcasing products they've browsed before or presenting new arrivals that align with their interests, this tailored approach keeps customers engaged and encourages them to explore further. By leveraging AI for personalization, you can create a more meaningful connection with your audience, turning casual browsers into loyal customers who feel a personal bond with your brand.

In advertising, AI demonstrates its prowess by optimizing spend and maximizing returns. Traditional advertising methods often involve a degree of guesswork, but AI changes the game by providing data-driven insights into campaign performance. AI-driven bid optimization tools analyze current market conditions and competitor activities to determine the best times and platforms to place ads. By adjusting bids in real-time, these tools ensure your advertising budget is spent efficiently, maximizing exposure without overspending. Real-time analytics provide a clear picture of your ads'performance, allowing you to make informed decisions on the fly. This enhances the effectiveness of your campaigns and ensures that your advertising dollars are invested where they will have the most significant impact. With AI guiding your advertising strategy, you can achieve better results with less waste, driving efficiency and profitability.

Social media platforms are bustling hubs of activity and insights, and AI helps you tap into this wealth of information. By monitoring social media trends and sentiments, AI tools can provide invaluable insights into what your audience is talking about and how they feel about your brand. Sentiment analysis tools scan social media conversations to gauge public opinion, identifying positive and negative sentiments that can inform your marketing strategies. Understanding these sentiments enables you to tailor your messaging to address customer concerns or capitalize on positive perceptions. Additionally, AI algorithms can identify key influencers within your industry, allowing you to collaborate with individuals who can amplify your brand's reach. By leveraging AI for social media insights, you better understand your audience, enabling more strategic and responsive marketing efforts. This strengthens your brand's presence and fosters a community of engaged and loyal followers who advocate for your brand.

3.3 FINANCIAL MANAGEMENT: USING AI FOR SMARTER DECISION-MAKING

Imagine sitting at your desk, surrounded by a sea of financial documents. Each paper represents hours of manual data entry and cross-checking, which are time-consuming and prone to errors. Now, picture AI is stepping into this scenario, transforming how financial reporting is done. AI can automate data extraction from these documents, instantly pulling relevant information and compiling it into coherent reports. This accelerates the reporting process and significantly reduces the likelihood of human error. Automated reconciliation processes streamline operations by matching transactions and resolving discrepancies with minimal human intervention. This efficiency allows you to focus on strategic financial planning rather than getting bogged down in the minutiae of data management.

When it comes to risk management, AI is an invaluable asset. Financial risks lurk in every corner of business, from fraudulent transactions to unstable market conditions. With its powerful algorithms, AI can detect real-time anomalies, flagging potential fraud before it escalates. These algorithms analyze patterns in financial data, identifying irregularities that might go unnoticed by the human eye. Additionally, AI-driven credit risk assessment tools evaluate the creditworthiness of potential clients or partners, offering comprehensive insights that inform your decision-making process. This proactive approach to risk management protects your assets and provides peace of mind, knowing that potential threats are being monitored continuously.

Managing cash flow effectively is the lifeblood of any business, and AI offers tools to optimize this critical task. Predictive cash flow analytics provide forecasts based on historical data and current financial trends, allowing you to anticipate and prepare for future financial needs. This foresight helps you manage receivables and payables more efficiently, ensuring your business remains financially healthy. Powered by AI, dynamic invoice processing further enhances cash flow management by automating invoice creation, sending, and tracking. This automation speeds up the invoicing process, reducing the time it takes to receive payments and improving liquidity. With AI in your financial toolkit, managing cash flow becomes a streamlined, efficient process, freeing up resources for growth and innovation.

Investment strategies benefit immensely from AI's data-driven insights. The financial markets are complex and ever-changing, but AI can confidently help navigate these waters. Portfolio optimization models analyze vast amounts of data to identify the best investment opportunities, balancing risk and return to align with your financial goals. These models consider a myriad of factors, from market trends to economic indicators, providing informed and strategic recommendations. AI also excels in predicting market trends, offering insights into potential shifts that could impact your investments. By leveraging these predictions, you can make informed decisions that enhance your investment portfolio'sperformance, ensuring that your financial strategies are robust and adaptable.

As we wrap up this chapter on practical AI applications in business, it's clear that AI is not just a tool but a catalyst for transformation. From optimizing customer service to revolutionizing financial management, AI offers solutions that drive efficiency, reduce costs, and enhance decision-making. These applications demonstrate AI's potential to reshape businesses, offering a competitive edge in today's fast-paced market. As we move into the next chapter, we'll explore how real-world companies successfully integrate AI, drawing lessons from their experiences to guide your journey in leveraging this powerful technology.

CHAPTER 4
Real-World Success Stories

I n a quaint town nestled along the coast, a small bakery named Sweet Sensations faced the challenge of keeping pace with customer demands without compromising its artisanal charm. Owners Emily and Jake were passionate about their craft but needed help with the daily grind of inventory management and customer service. Enter AI, a tool they initially thought was reserved for tech giants. Adopting open-source AI software transformed their operations without draining their finances. The AI system streamlined inventory checks, predicting when supplies would run low and automatically placing orders, thus ensuring they never ran out of their most beloved pastries. This cost-effective solution, accessible and affordable, allowed them to focus on what they did best—baking delicious treats. Their story is a testament to how small businesses can leverage technology to overcome operational hurdles and thrive in competitive markets.

The journey of AI integration doesn't have to be an all-or-nothing endeavor. Many small businesses have succeeded through incremental adoption, gradually incorporating AI to enhance their operations. Consider a local retail store that began its AI journey by automating simple customer service tasks. Initially, they deployed a chatbot to handle after-hours inquiries, which improved customer satisfaction and freed up staff to focus on in-store assistance during peak hours. As the business grew more comfortable with AI, it expanded its use to analyze sales data and refine its marketing strategies. By taking a step-by-step approach, the store owner could see measurable customer engagement and sales improvements without overwhelming their team or resources. This gradual integration showcases how businesses can build momentum, achieving significant gains with manageable changes.

When resources are limited, creativity becomes an entrepreneur's greatest asset. Small businesses have demonstrated remarkable resourcefulness in AI integration, often finding innovative ways to implement technology without breaking the bank. One effective strategy is cross-training employees on AI tools, enabling them to wear multiple hats and maximize the utility of available technology. This approach empowers staff to take ownership of AI projects, fostering a culture of innovation and adaptability. Another strategy involves collaborating with local tech startups, which can provide technical expertise and support in exchange for real-world testing opportunities. Such partnerships help businesses implement AI effectively and strengthen community ties, creating a network of mutual support and growth. Small businesses can overcome financial constraints by exploring unconventional solutions and achieving technological advancements that propel them forward.

Case Study: AI in Action

A charming café in the city's heart provides a vivid example of AI's transformative power. Faced with the dual challenges of managing inventory and minimizing waste, the café owner turned to AI for a solution. By implementing AI-driven inventory management software, they gained insights into consumption patterns, allowing them to adjust orders in real time. This precision reduced food waste significantly, reinvesting cost savings into enhancing the customer experience. Meanwhile, a boutique retailer across town harnessed AI for personalized customer recommendations. By analyzing purchase data, the AI system suggested products tailored to individual customer preferences, increasing customer satisfaction and sales. These examples underscore the potential of AI to drive efficiency and growth, even for businesses operating within tight budgets.

The success of these small businesses highlights the potential for AI to revolutionize operations, driving both efficiency and cost savings. They have implemented sophisticated AI solutions by leveraging open-source software and cloud-based services without incurring prohibitive costs. The incremental approach to AI adoption has allowed them to see tangible benefits while maintaining operational stability. Moreover, their resourceful strategies, such as employee cross-training and partnerships with tech startups, have enabled them to overcome resource constraints and fully realize the advantages of AI technology. These real-world success stories are powerful reminders that small businesses can harness AI to achieve remarkable outcomes with little ingenuity and the right tools.

4.1 INDUSTRY-SPECIFIC WINS: TAILORED AI APPLICATIONS

AI has been a transformative force in the vast healthcare landscape, particularly in diagnostics. Hospitals and clinics increasingly adopt AI-enhanced diagnostic tools that analyze medical images precisely and quickly. These tools apply complex algorithms to scan X-rays, MRIs, and CT scans, identifying anomalies that might be missed by the human eye. This technology accelerates diagnosis and enhances accuracy, leading to better patient outcomes. For instance, AI systems can detect early signs of diseases like cancer, allowing for timely intervention and treatment. By tailoring AI to meet the specific needs of healthcare professionals, these tools are revolutionizing patient care and making diagnostics more accessible and efficient.

The finance industry is another sector reaping the benefits of AI, mainly through AI-driven trading algorithms. These algorithms process vast amounts of data at lightning speed, identifying trading opportunities that align with market trends and patterns. By analyzing historical data and current market conditions, AI can accurately predict stock movements, providing traders with valuable insights that inform their strategies. This capability enhances decision-making and reduces the risk of human error. Moreover, AI's ability to process data in real time allows for more agile trading, enabling financial institutions to stay ahead in a competitive market. By customizing AI applications to fit the unique demands of finance, businesses can optimize their trading activities, ultimately driving profitability and growth.

AI's versatility shines across many industries, each benefiting from its adaptability to specific needs. AI is making waves in real estate by offering sophisticated market analysis tools. These tools evaluate property values, neighborhood trends, and investment potential, providing realtors and investors with comprehensive insights that guide their decisions. Similarly, AI in agriculture drives precision farming techniques, where sensors and drones collect data on soil health, crop conditions, and weather patterns. This information enables farmers to optimize resource use and boost yields, contributing to sustainable farming practices. Education, too, is embracing AI through personalized learning platforms that tailor educational content to individual students' needs. By analyzing learning patterns and preferences, AI helps educators provide customized experiences that enhance student engagement and success. These diverse use cases demonstrate AI'sability to adapt to different contexts, delivering solutions that address each industry's unique challenges.

Successful AI deployment often hinges on a few common factors that transcend industry boundaries. Strong leadership and vision are crucial, as they set the tone for innovation and drive AI initiatives forward. Leaders who embrace AI as a strategic tool inspire their teams to explore new possibilities and push boundaries. Effective change management strategies also play a pivotal role in ensuring smooth integration. By fostering a culture of adaptability and continuous learning, businesses can confidently navigate the complexities of AI adoption. This approach mitigates resistance to change and encourages employees to embrace new technologies, leveraging AI to its full potential. Through strategic planning and execution, organizations can unlock the transformative power of AI, reaping the benefits of innovation and growth.

Insights from industry leaders who have successfully implemented AI further illuminate the path to success. In an interview, the CEO of a leading tech company described AI as a "game-changer" that has redefined their approach to innovation. Integrating AI across their operations has streamlined processes, enhanced customer experiences, and driven revenue growth. Similarly, operational managers from various sectors have shared testimonials on AI's impact, highlighting improved efficiency, accuracy, and decision-making. These firsthand accounts underscore the tangible benefits of AI, offering valuable lessons for businesses looking to embark on their AI journey. By learning from those who have successfully navigated the challenges of AI integration, entrepreneurs can gain the insights needed to implement effective strategies and achieve their objectives.

4.2 FROM STARTUPS TO GIANTS: SCALING WITH AI

In startups, the ability to scale efficiently can be the difference between success and stagnation. Many have found that AI offers a unique advantage, particularly in customer acquisition strategies. By leveraging AI-driven data analytics, startups can precisely target potential customers with personalized marketing campaigns, optimizing their reach and engagement. For instance, a budding tech company used AI to analyze market trends and consumer behavior, allowing them to tailor their outreach and convert leads more effectively. This strategic use of AI boosted their customer base and set the stage for sustainable growth.

Beyond customer acquisition, AI is crucial in automating backend processes, which is fundamental to scaling operations. As startups transition into larger markets, managing increased data volumes and operational demands becomes challenging. AI solutions streamline these processes, handling everything from inventory management to logistical coordination with minimal human intervention. An example is a logistics startup that utilized AI to automate its supply chain, enabling it to expand its operations globally without a proportional increase in staff. This automation allowed them to maintain high efficiency and service quality, even as their customer base and geographical reach expanded. Such scalable AI solutions reduce operational costs and ensure startups can handle growth seamlessly.

Many companies have experienced dramatic growth trajectories with the support of AI, showcasing its potential to transform businesses. Consider a tech startup that initially operated within a regional market. By integrating AI-based logistics into their operations, they could easily optimize delivery routes and manage international shipments. This capability facilitated their expansion into global markets, significantly increasing their revenue and market share. Similarly, an e-commerce company harnessed AI-powered personalization to enhance the shopping experience, tailoring product recommendations to individual customers. This personalization boosted customer loyalty and sales, propelling the company to the forefront of its industry. These examples illustrate how AI can catalyze growth, empowering companies to scale rapidly and efficiently.

The competitive landscape of modern business demands that companies differentiate themselves, and AI has proven to be a key differentiator. AI enables businesses to implement competitive pricing strategies in highly competitive environments by analyzing real-time market data and consumer demand. This allows companies to adjust prices dynamically, ensuring they remain competitive without sacrificing margins. Additionally, AI accelerates product development cycles by providing insights into consumer preferences and market trends. Companies can leverage these insights to refine their offerings more quickly, staying ahead of competitors and capturing market share. By integrating AI into their strategic planning, businesses enhance their competitive advantage and position themselves for long-term success.

Scaling with AI has its challenges, but the technology offers solutions to overcome them. As companies grow, managing the influx of data becomes increasingly complex. AI helps by efficiently processing and analyzing vast amounts of information, providing actionable insights that inform business decisions. For example, a growing retail chain used AI to manage its expanding inventory across multiple locations, optimizing stock levels and reducing waste. Additionally, international operations present unique challenges, such as navigating diverse regulatory environments and coordinating global logistics. AI streamlines these operations by automating compliance checks and optimizing cross-border supply chains, ensuring smooth international expansion. Businesses can scale confidently by addressing these challenges with AI, leveraging technology to overcome obstacles and drive growth.

4.3 LESSONS LEARNED: WHAT WORKED AND WHAT DIDN'T

Reflecting on AI's successful implementations reveals the importance of iterative testing and adaptation. One key takeaway is that businesses that embrace a flexible approach to AI projects often see more tremendous success. By continuously testing and refining AI systems, these companies can adjust strategies based on real-world feedback, ensuring the technology remains aligned with their evolving needs. This adaptability allows businesses to pivot quickly, addressing unforeseen challenges before they escalate. Furthermore, aligning AI projects with overarching business goals is crucial. Companies that integrate AI within the framework of their strategic objectives generally achieve better cohesion and effectiveness. This alignment ensures that AI initiatives are not isolated technology experiments but integral components of a broader business plan, driving value and supporting long-term growth.

However, not all AI journeys are smooth. Common pitfalls often arise from over-reliance on technology without adequate human oversight. It's easy to fall into the trap of thinking that AI can solve all problems independently. Yet, AI systems can make better decisions with human input, especially in areas requiring nuanced understanding. Ignoring data quality and governance issues is another frequent mistake. AI systems are only as good as the data they process. Inadequate data management can lead to inaccurate insights and misguided strategies. Successful AI implementations require robust data governance frameworks that ensure data integrity and security, enabling systems to function optimally. Addressing these pitfalls involves balancing the technological capabilities of AI with human insight and maintaining rigorous data standards.

Drawing from these insights, several actionable recommendations emerge for future AI initiatives. First, establishing clear metrics for AI success is vital. Defining what success looks like for each project helps teams focus on specific outcomes and measure progress accurately. These metrics should be aligned with business objectives and regularly reviewed to remain relevant. Additionally, fostering a culture of continuous learning and improvement is essential. Encouraging teams to stay updated with AI advancements and to experiment with new approaches can lead to innovative solutions and improved performance. By creating an environment that values learning and adaptation, businesses can remain agile and responsive to changing market dynamics, leveraging AI to its full potential.

Despite the promise of AI, some projects need to meet expectations. Stories of underperformance often highlight a lack of stakeholder engagement as a critical factor. When key stakeholders are not involved from the start, projects can lose direction or face resistance, hindering progress. Ensuring stakeholders are engaged and supportive throughout the AI project lifecycle is crucial for success. Misalignment between AI capabilities and business needs can also lead to disappointing outcomes. AI projects that fail to address specific business challenges or align with strategic goals often need help to deliver value. This misalignment underscores the importance of understanding the business's unique needs and selecting AI solutions that directly address those needs. Learning from these failures involves ensuring that AI projects are not only technically sound but also strategically relevant, with clear support from all stakeholders.

As we look at the bigger picture, these lessons learned provide a framework for navigating the complexities of AI integration. Businesses can harness AI'spotential effectively by focusing on iterative testing, aligning projects with business goals, and avoiding common pitfalls. With clear metrics and a culture of continuous learning, companies can stay ahead of the curve, confidently adapting to new challenges and opportunities. These insights connect to the broader theme of innovation and adaptability, setting the stage for exploring how AI can drive transformative change across various business landscapes.

CHAPTER 5

Overcoming Common Pain Points

A s the sun set over the bustling streets of New York, a small business owner named Alex sat at his desk, surrounded by the remnants of a long day. Despite his best efforts, Alex felt overwhelmed by the complexities of integrating artificial intelligence into his operations. He knew that AI could revolutionize his business, yet the path seemed fraught with challenges. Many entrepreneurs like Alex share this sentiment, recognizing the transformative power of AI but grappling with the practicalities of implementation. This chapter aims to demystify the process, offering step-by-step guidance to simplify AI integration and address common pain points faced by business owners eager to harness the potential of this powerful technology.

5.1 SIMPLIFYING AI INTEGRATION: STEP-BY-STEP ROADMAPS

Integrating AI into your business requires a clear plan to minimize complexity and risk. Start by conducting an initial assessment to identify areas where AI can add value. This involves setting concrete goals that align with your business objectives, such as improving customer service or streamlining operations. Once your goals are established, pilot projects are valuable testing ground. Begin with a small-scale implementation to evaluate the effectiveness of AI solutions in a controlled environment. This allows you to gather insights, refine strategies, and build confidence before committing to a full rollout. Evaluating pilot projects provides a clear picture of how AI can impact your business, enabling you to make informed decisions about scaling up.

Adopting modular AI systems can further ease the integration process. These systems are designed to be implemented incrementally, allowing you to introduce AI components gradually without overwhelming your existing infrastructure. Picture plug-and-play AI components that can be seamlessly integrated into your operations. This modular approach reduces upfront costs and provides flexibility, enabling you to expand AI capabilities as your business grows. Incremental testing and deployment ensure that each new component is thoroughly vetted, minimizing disruptions and maximizing benefits. By taking it one step at a time, you can build a robust AI infrastructure that evolves alongside your business, adapting to changing needs and opportunities.

Managing organizational change is crucial for smooth AI integration. Change can be daunting, but with practical strategies, it becomes manageable. Start by developing communication plans to engage stakeholders at every process stage. Transparency is critical, as it helps build trust and buy-in from your team. Regular updates and open forums for discussion allow stakeholders to voice concerns and contribute to the integration process. Training programs are another essential component, equipping employees with the skills to adapt to new AI systems. These programs should be tailored to your team's needs, focusing on practical applications and hands-on experience. Investing in change management creates an environment where AI is embraced as a tool for innovation, fostering a culture of collaboration and continuous improvement.

Regularly reviewing and adjusting integration strategies based on feedback and outcomes is vital to ensure long-term success. Establish key performance indicators (KPIs) to measure the effectiveness of AI solutions against your initial goals. These KPIs provide valuable insights into areas of success and opportunities for improvement. Implement feedback loops that encourage ongoing team communication, allowing real-time strategy adjustments. Creating a continuous evaluation culture ensures that AI solutions remain relevant and impactful, driving sustained growth and innovation. This proactive approach addresses potential challenges and empowers your business to adapt to changing market dynamics, maintaining a competitive edge in an ever-evolving landscape.

Reflection Section: Crafting Your Integration Plan

Take a moment to reflect on your business's current operations and identify areas where AI could make a meaningful impact. Consider the following questions: What specific challenges are you facing that AI could address? How can AI solutions align with your strategic goals? What resources and support will be needed for successful integration? Use these reflections to develop a clear integration plan that sets the stage for successful AI adoption. Remember, the goal is to create a roadmap that guides your business through the complexities of AI, transforming challenges into opportunities for growth and innovation.

5.2 BRIDGING THE SKILLS GAP: TRAINING AND RESOURCES FOR ENTREPRENEURS

In AI adoption, understanding the necessary skills is a foundational step. It's akin to building a house—you need a solid base before anything else. The cornerstone of this foundation is a basic understanding of AI concepts. Entrepreneurs and their teams should grasp what AI truly is, its capabilities, and its limitations. This knowledge demystifies the technology, making it more approachable and less intimidating. Beyond these basics, data analysis and interpretation skills become crucial. AI thrives on data, turning raw numbers into actionable insights. Understanding how to interpret these insights is critical to making informed decisions that align with business goals. This skill set, while technical, is increasingly accessible thanks to user-friendly tools and platforms designed with non-experts in mind.

Comprehensive training programs should be a priority to bridge the gap between current capabilities and the skills needed for AI. Start with online AI certification courses. These courses offer flexibility, allowing employees to learn at their own pace while gaining valuable credentials. Platforms like Coursera and edX provide a range of courses tailored to different levels of expertise, from beginner to advanced. Workshops on AI tools and applications are also beneficial, offering hands-on experience that reinforces theoretical knowledge. These workshops can be conducted in-house or through external providers, focusing on the practical application of AI in your specific industry. By investing in training, you enhance your team's capabilities and foster a culture of curiosity and growth, encouraging employees to explore new technologies and their potential benefits.

Creating a learning environment that encourages continuous development is vital to keeping pace with AI advancements. Internal knowledge-sharing sessions are an effective way to promote this culture. These sessions allow employees to share insights and experiences, fostering collaboration and innovation. They also provide a platform for discussing AI trends and developments, keeping everyone informed and engaged. Incentives for skill development, such as recognition programs or financial bonuses, can further motivate employees to pursue learning opportunities. By valuing and rewarding continuous learning, you create an atmosphere where innovation thrives and employees feel empowered to contribute to the company's success. This approach benefits individual growth and drives the organization forward, ensuring it remains agile and competitive in an ever-evolving landscape.

External partnerships can be instrumental in supporting skill development and providing access to resources and expertise that might not be available internally. Collaborating with local universities can offer structured learning opportunities, such as courses, workshops, or certification programs. These institutions often have cutting-edge research and access to the latest technologies, allowing your team to learn from leading experts in the field. Internships and mentorship programs with tech firms are another valuable resource, providing practical experience and insights into AI applications. These partnerships can bridge the gap between academic knowledge and real-world application, giving employees a comprehensive understanding of AI's potential. By leveraging external partnerships, you expand your team's learning opportunities, ensuring they have the skills to navigate AI's complexities with confidence and competence.

5.3 BUDGET-FRIENDLY AI: COST-EFFECTIVE TOOLS AND STRATEGIES

In the bustling world of entrepreneurship, finding budget-friendly solutions is often the key to success. Many entrepreneurs assume that the cost will be prohibitive when it comes to AI. However, open-source AI software offers a compelling alternative, minimizing expenses without sacrificing functionality. Tools like TensorFlow, a robust machine learning framework, provide the flexibility to develop complex models without the hefty price tag. TensorFlow's broad adoption in the industry means there's a vast community ready to offer support and share insights, making it an ideal choice for businesses eager to dive into AI. Similarly, Apache Mahout provides scalable algorithms for machine learning, helping companies to process large datasets efficiently. You can explore AI's transformative potential by leveraging these open-source tools without stretching your budget too thin.

Cloud-based AI solutions further democratize access to advanced technology, offering flexibility and scalability at a fraction of traditional costs. Services like AWS Machine Learning and Google Cloud AI tools provide powerful computing capabilities without the need for significant upfront investments in hardware. These platforms operate on a pay-as-you-go basis, allowing businesses to scale resources according to their needs. This model is particularly advantageous for startups and small businesses, where budget constraints often limit access to cutting-edge technology. With cloud-based AI, you can experiment and innovate without committing to large capital expenditures. Moreover, integrating disparate data sets in the cloud facilitates rapid analysis and deeper insights, enabling real-time decision-making that can propel your business forward.

The pay-as-you-go pricing model is a game-changer for entrepreneurs looking to effectively manage and predict AI-related expenses. This approach allows you to subscribe to AI services or utilize resources based on usage, offering a transparent and predictable cost structure. Subscription-based AI services provide access to the latest advancements and updates, ensuring your technology remains competitive without needing costly upgrades. On the other hand, usage-based pricing allows you to pay only for the resources consumed, making it easy to adjust spending according to your budget. This flexibility is invaluable for businesses experiencing seasonal fluctuations or rapid growth, as it ensures that AI capabilities can be scaled up or down as needed, optimizing resource utilization and minimizing waste.

Integrating AI solutions efficiently often means maximizing existing resources within your business. Many organizations already utilize CRM systems to manage customer relationships, and these platforms can be enhanced with AI capabilities to boost productivity and insights. Integrating AI tools with your CRM allows you to automate routine tasks, streamline processes, and gain valuable insights into customer behavior. Similarly, ERP systems, which manage core business processes, can be augmented with AI to enhance decision-making and operational efficiency. This approach maximizes the value of current investments and facilitates a smoother transition to AI, reducing the need for additional infrastructure or radical changes. By leveraging what you already have, you can introduce AI cost-effectively and seamlessly, positioning your business for success in a competitive market.

As you explore the world of AI, consider the multitude of open-source and cloud-based solutions available. These tools and platforms offer a cost-effective means to harness AI's power, enabling you to innovate and compete without breaking the bank. By adopting a strategic approach that leverages existing resources and flexible pricing models, you can integrate AI into your operations to align with your budget and business goals. This democratizes access to advanced technology and empowers you to drive growth and efficiency, ensuring that your business remains agile and competitive in an ever-evolving landscape.

5.4 FUTURE-PROOFING YOUR BUSINESS: KEEPING UP WITH AI ADVANCEMENTS

In the rapidly evolving world of AI, staying informed is not just beneficial—it's crucial. Consider following AI thought leaders and publications to keep abreast of the latest developments. Industry experts often find that sharing insights on LinkedIn or Twitter offers valuable perspectives to guide your strategies. Publications like MIT Technology Review and WIRED provide in-depth analyses of emerging trends and technologies, helping you anticipate shifts that could impact your business. Attending AI conferences and webinars is another effective way to stay updated. These events connect you with innovators and peers, offering a front-row seat to the latest breakthroughs and networking opportunities that can lead to strategic partnerships. By immersing yourself in these resources, you position your business to adapt and thrive amidst technological advancements.

Investing in agile technologies ensures your business can evolve alongside AI innovations. Agile project management frameworks, such as Scrum or Kanban, provide flexibility and allow for quick adaptation. These frameworks emphasize iterative development and continuous feedback, allowing your team to respond promptly to new information and shifting priorities. Alongside agile methodologies, adopting flexible tech architectures is equally essential. Cloud-based solutions, for instance, offer scalability and adaptability, enabling you to adjust resources as needed without extensive reconfiguration. Such architectures support the rapid integration of new AI tools and applications, ensuring your infrastructure can accommodate evolving demands. By prioritizing agility in process and technology, you create a resilient foundation supporting sustained growth and innovation.

Promoting a culture of strategic innovation within your organization encourages experimentation with new AI technologies. Research and development initiatives dedicated to AI exploration can uncover novel applications and processes that enhance your competitive edge. Establishing innovation labs within your company provides a dedicated space for creative problem-solving and prototyping, fostering an environment where ideas can flourish. These labs are incubators for testing and refining AI-driven solutions, encouraging cross-disciplinary collaboration and knowledge sharing. By championing innovation, you empower your team to push boundaries and explore possibilities, driving transformative change that positions your business at the forefront of your industry.

Regular evaluation and adaptation of AI strategies are vital to maintain a competitive edge in an ever-changing landscape. Conducting performance reviews of your AI initiatives allows you to assess their impact and identify areas for improvement. Strategic adjustments based on these insights ensure that your AI efforts align with your business objectives and market dynamics. Scenario planning for AI-driven changes further enhances your ability to navigate uncertainty. You can proactively develop strategies to address challenges and seize opportunities by envisioning potential future scenarios and their implications. This ongoing process of refinement and adaptation ensures the continued relevance of your AI initiatives and positions your business to capitalize on emerging trends and technologies.

Interactive Element: AI Trend Tracker

Consider creating an AI Trend Tracker to inform your team about the latest developments. This could be a shared document or digital board where team members can post articles, insights, and updates related to AI advancements. Encourage everyone to contribute, fostering a culture of continuous learning and collaboration. Regularly reviewing and discussing these updates in team meetings can spark new ideas and strategies, ensuring your business remains at the cutting edge of innovation.

As you build a future-ready enterprise, remember that adaptability and innovation are your allies when navigating the AI landscape. You ensure your business remains resilient and competitive by staying informed, investing in agile technologies, fostering innovation, and continuously evaluating your strategies. These practices not only future-proof your operations but also empower you to lead confidently into the next chapter of AI-driven growth.

CHAPTER 6

Measuring AI Impact and ROI

In the heart of Silicon Valley, a startup named BrightTech found its footing by harnessing AI to revolutionize data management. The founder, Lisa, recognized early on that she needed to measure its impact accurately to truly leverage AI's potential. She wasn't alone in this realization. Across industries, the ability to quantify AI's success has become crucial for businesses eager to justify investments and align AI initiatives with broader objectives. As you delve into this chapter, you'll discover that establishing and tailoring key performance indicators (KPIs) is fundamental to understanding AI's effectiveness. Focusing on metrics reflecting your business goals can transform data into actionable insights, driving growth and innovation.

Defining relevant KPIs begins with a clear understanding of your business objectives. Whether enhancing customer satisfaction or boosting operational efficiency, KPIs should mirror these goals, offering a tangible measure of AI's contribution. For instance, customer satisfaction scores can reflect how AI-driven interfaces improve user interactions, while operational efficiency metrics might track how automation reduces process time. These indicators highlight AI's direct impact and guide strategic decisions, ensuring that technology investments align with your vision for growth. By establishing KPIs that resonate with your core objectives, you create a framework that supports continuous improvement and informed decision-making, positioning your business for success in an AI-driven world.

Tailoring KPIs to specific AI applications is equally important. Each AI initiative serves unique purposes; your metrics should reflect these nuances. For example, if your AI application focuses on streamlining processes, time savings from automation might be a key metric. Similarly, if increasing sales through personalized marketing is your goal, revenue growth driven by AI insights is a pertinent KPI. Customizing your performance indicators gives you a clearer picture of how each AI component contributes to your business objectives. This tailored approach enhances the accuracy of your evaluations and provides the insights needed to optimize AI applications continually. As AI technologies evolve, revisiting and refining these KPIs ensures they remain relevant and reflect your strategic goals.

Real-time analytics are pivotal in monitoring KPIs, offering invaluable insights that drive agile decision-making. Live dashboards provide instant access to critical metrics, enabling you to track performance as it unfolds. This immediate visibility allows for timely interventions, whether adjusting marketing strategies or reallocating resources to address operational bottlenecks. Moreover, real-time alerts notify you of significant deviations in KPI performance, prompting swift action to mitigate risks or capitalize on emerging opportunities. By leveraging real-time data, you can maintain a proactive stance, ensuring that your AI initiatives remain aligned with business objectives and responsive to changing market dynamics. You cultivate an environment where agility and innovation thrive, propelling your business toward sustained success.

Benchmarking KPI performance against industry standards provides a valuable perspective on your AI initiatives' success. By comparing your metrics to those of peers and competitors, you gain insights into your relative performance and identify areas for improvement. Industry-specific KPI benchmarks offer a reference point for evaluating your achievements, highlighting strengths, and uncovering potential gaps. Competitive analysis further enriches this process, revealing how your AI solutions stack up against those of market leaders. This comparative approach informs strategic adjustments and inspires innovation, driving your AI initiatives to new heights. As you measure and refine your KPIs, benchmarking serves as both a mirror and a motivator, challenging you to strive for excellence and positioning your business as a leader in AI-driven innovation.

Interactive Element: KPI Tracking Template

Consider using a KPI tracking template to facilitate your journey in measuring AI impact. This tool helps organize and visualize your performance metrics, ensuring you stay on top of your AI initiatives. Set up columns for each KPI, including customer satisfaction scores and operational efficiency metrics. Track time savings and revenue growth alongside industry benchmarks, updating the template with real-time data to capture a comprehensive view of your progress. This visual aid simplifies monitoring and empowers you to make informed decisions that align with your strategic goals.

6.1 CALCULATING ROI: JUSTIFYING AI INVESTMENTS

Imagine a bustling manufacturing plant on the edge of town. Before implementing AI, the plant was a hive of activity, yet inefficiencies lurked beneath the surface. Establishing a baseline is crucial here. You create a reference point by capturing pre-implementation performance metrics, such as labor costs and production error rates. This historical data analysis is your compass, guiding you in measuring AI's impact. With it, improvements post-AI would remain tangible, like comparing apples to oranges. With a solid baseline, you gain clarity, allowing you to quantify changes and assess AI's actual value. It's akin to having a map before a road trip, ensuring you know where you started and how far you've traveled.

AI's potential to reduce costs is significant. Automation often leads to reduced labor costs, freeing up resources for strategic initiatives. Imagine AI-powered machines handling repetitive tasks, allowing your human workforce to focus on innovation. This shift doesn't just save money; it enhances productivity. Then, there's the revenue growth from AI-driven marketing. AI can identify trends and preferences by analyzing customer data, enabling more targeted campaigns. This precision boosts sales, turning potential leads into loyal customers. Additionally, AI reduces production errors, enhancing quality and reducing waste. These elements contribute to a healthier bottom line, reflecting AI's multifaceted value in tangible financial terms.

Yet, some benefits of AI extend beyond the numbers. Improved customer experience, for instance, is a powerful intangible benefit. AI can personalize interactions and predict needs, enhancing satisfaction and loyalty. This improved customer loyalty often translates into repeat business, a revenue stream that's difficult to quantify but invaluable. Furthermore, an enhanced market position is another intangible gain. By adopting cutting-edge technology, your brand is perceived as innovative and forward-thinking. This perception can translate into competitive advantage, attracting new customers and partners eager to align with innovation leaders. These intangible benefits often lay the groundwork for long-term success, creating a ripple effect bolsters reputation and market standing.

A comprehensive ROI framework considers all these factors. Begin with ROI calculation formulas. The basic formula—ROI equals net gain from investment divided by investment cost, multiplied by 100—provides a starting point. But scenarios vary, and so should your calculations. Use scenario analysis to project different ROI outcomes based on various conditions, such as scaling operations or expanding into new markets. This approach ensures you capture the full spectrum of AI's potential impact. While numbers tell part of the story, a detailed framework reveals the nuances, capturing both immediate gains and long-term strategic advantages. Considering these diverse elements, you create a robust foundation for evaluating AI's contribution to your business strategy.

Visual Element: ROI Calculator

Consider using an ROI calculator to assist in your evaluations:

1. Consider.
2. Input your baseline metrics, anticipated cost savings, and projected revenue gains to visualize potential returns. This tool can help clarify the financial impact of AI investments, guiding your strategic decisions with data-driven insights.
3. Use it to explore various scenarios, adjusting parameters to reflect growth trajectories and investment strategies.

This dynamic approach empowers you to make informed decisions, maximizing AI's potential while aligning with your business objectives.

6.2 CONTINUOUS IMPROVEMENT: ITERATING AI STRATEGIES

In the dynamic realm of artificial intelligence, the ability to adapt and refine strategies is paramount. To achieve this, a feedback loop system becomes an invaluable tool. Imagine an ongoing conversation where data and insights continuously inform your AI initiatives. One way to gather real-time input on AI performance is to implement customer feedback mechanisms. For instance, after a customer interacts with your AI-driven service, soliciting feedback can reveal how well the AI meets their needs or where improvements are necessary. This direct line to your customers provides insights that can drive meaningful enhancements. Employee input is equally crucial. Those who work with AI systems daily can offer unique perspectives on what's working and what's not. Regular team meetings or anonymous surveys can uncover insights from your workforce, providing a holistic view of AI's impact and areas ripe for improvement.

Regularly reviewing AI performance against your objectives and KPIs is akin to a health check-up for your AI systems. Monthly audits can offer a snapshot of AI's effectiveness, allowing you to identify deviations from anticipated outcomes. These audits will enable you to analyze the data and see where your AI strategies need improvement. Complementing this with quarterly strategic reviews gives you a broader perspective, allowing you to align AI performance with long-term business goals. These reviews serve as a crucial checkpoint, ensuring your AI initiatives align with evolving business priorities and market conditions. This periodic assessment highlights successes and pinpoints areas for refinement, driving continuous improvement and innovation across your organization.

Agile methodologies prove beneficial in iteratively adapting AI strategies and processes. Think of agile as a mindset that embraces flexibility and responsiveness. Sprint planning, a cornerstone of agile, allows you to break down AI projects into manageable tasks with set timelines. These short, focused bursts of work enable rapid prototyping of AI solutions, facilitating quick feedback and adjustment. By embracing this iterative process, you create a constant learning and adaptation cycle, ensuring that AI solutions evolve in response to real-world challenges and opportunities. This approach accelerates development and reduces risks, as you can quickly pivot based on insights gleaned from each sprint. Agile adaptation fosters a culture of resilience and innovation, empowering your team to stay ahead in a rapidly changing technological landscape.

Encouraging experimentation and innovation is the lifeblood of staying competitive in the AI arena. By fostering an environment where new ideas are welcomed and tested, you open the door to groundbreaking advancements. Pilot programs for emerging AI tools offer a sandbox for exploring potential applications. These programs allow you to test new technologies on a small scale before committing to full implementation, minimizing risk while maximizing learning. Innovation contests within your organization can also spark creativity and collaboration. By challenging teams to develop novel AI solutions, you tap into the collective ingenuity of your workforce. This drives engagement and surfaces innovative approaches that might otherwise go unnoticed. The spirit of experimentation breeds a culture of curiosity and discovery, propelling your AI initiatives toward uncharted territories with confidence and excitement.

6.3 COMMUNICATING SUCCESS: SHARING AI WINS WITH STAKEHOLDERS

In business, the ability to effectively communicate the success of AI initiatives is crucial. Crafting a compelling narrative highlighting AI's impact can transform your stakeholders' perceptions and foster enthusiasm for future projects. Imagine presenting a story where AI transformed routine processes into streamlined operations, enhancing productivity and profitability. You can draw your audience into the narrative by employing storytelling techniques, illustrating how AI initiatives have driven tangible business impacts. Incorporate real-world examples and case studies that showcase AI achievements, such as a retail company using AI to optimize inventory management, resulting in significant cost savings and customer satisfaction. These stories capture attention and provide concrete evidence of AI's value, making the case for continued investment and support.

Visual elements are pivotal in conveying complex data in an accessible manner. Infographics, for instance, can vividly depict improvements in KPIs, illustrating AI's impact at a glance. Consider a chart demonstrating how AI reduced processing times, with clear bars showing before-and-after scenarios. Such visual comparisons simplify understanding and emphasize the extent of AI's contributions. Presenting data visually enhances comprehension and leaves a lasting impression, reinforcing the narrative of success. Visuals transform abstract numbers into concrete insights, facilitating better communication with diverse audiences, from executives to frontline employees.

Tailoring communication to meet different stakeholder groups' specific interests and concerns ensures your message resonates effectively. When addressing leadership teams, concise executive summaries can highlight strategic gains and align AI outcomes with the company's goals. These summaries distill complex information into key points, giving leaders the insights they need to make informed decisions. For IT departments, detailed technical reports that delve into the nuts and bolts of AI technology can foster understanding and facilitate collaboration. This tailored approach ensures that each stakeholder group receives relevant information, promoting engagement and support across the organization.

Emphasizing strategic alignment in your communications is essential. You underscore their relevance and importance by showcasing how AI initiatives align with broader organizational goals. Strategic goal alignment presentations can highlight the synergy between AI projects and the company's long-term vision, reinforcing the strategic value of AI. Additionally, crafting long-term vision statements that include AI contributions can inspire confidence and commitment from stakeholders, demonstrating that AI is not just a short-term solution but a vital component of the company's future success. By highlighting how AI fits into the bigger picture, you foster a sense of purpose and direction, ensuring stakeholders understand AI's role in driving the organization forward.

In the next chapter, we will explore how to address ethical and security concerns related to AI, ensuring responsible use and trust in these transformative technologies.

CHAPTER 7

Addressing Ethical and Security Concerns

I n today's fast-paced digital era, artificial intelligence (AI) is not just a tool for innovation but a catalyst for transformation across industries. However, ethical considerations are paramount as AI becomes more integrated into business operations. Imagine a world where AI systems make decisions that impact lives daily, from healthcare to finance. This reality underscores the importance of ethical AI principles, which ensure AI applications are fair, accountable, and transparent. These principles guide the development of AI technologies and build trust with stakeholders, fostering environments where AI acts responsibly.

At the heart of ethical AI lies fairness in decision-making. AI systems must operate without bias, offering equitable outcomes for all users. Unfortunately, bias can creep into AI through the data used for training. For example, the AI system can perpetuate existing inequalities if a dataset lacks diversity. To combat this, ensuring datasets are representative and inclusive is crucial. Regular audits and algorithmic fairness checks can identify and mitigate biases, ensuring AI systems are just and impartial. These efforts support ethical AI development and align with broader societal values of equality and justice.

Transparency in AI algorithms is another cornerstone of ethical AI. Users must understand how AI systems reach decisions, mainly when those decisions affect people's lives. By providing clear explanations of AI processes, businesses can demystify the "black box" of AI, fostering trust and confidence among users. Transparency also makes AI documentation publicly accessible, allowing stakeholders to examine and verify AI operations. This openness enhances accountability and aligns with increasing regulatory demands for AI clarity and transparency.

Accountability frameworks for AI use are essential for maintaining ethical standards. Businesses must establish clear guidelines and responsibilities for AI deployment, ensuring that AI systems operate within defined ethical boundaries. These frameworks should include mechanisms for monitoring AI performance and addressing any moral concerns. By holding AI systems accountable for their actions, businesses can prevent misuse and ensure AI contributes positively to society.

Promoting responsible AI development from the outset is vital. This involves incorporating ethical guidelines into AI development, ensuring that moral considerations are not an afterthought. Engaging stakeholders, including developers, users, and policymakers, in AI development discussions can provide diverse perspectives and insights. This collaborative approach ensures that AI systems are designed with a comprehensive understanding of potential ethical implications. By prioritizing ethics in development, businesses can create AI solutions that are not only innovative but also socially responsible and aligned with human values.

To encourage ethical AI use, businesses should adopt codes of conduct that outline acceptable AI practices. These codes serve as a reference point for employees and stakeholders, guiding ethical AI implementation and use. Establishing ethical review boards can further support this effort by providing oversight and guidance on AI projects. These boards can assess AI applications for ethical compliance, offering recommendations to ensure AI systems adhere to ethical standards and best practices. By embedding ethics into the organizational culture, businesses can foster an environment where ethical AI use is the norm, not the exception.

Reflection Section: Ethical AI Assessment

Consider conducting an ethical AI assessment within your organization. Review your current AI applications and evaluate them against ethical principles such as fairness, transparency, and accountability. Identify areas where improvements are needed and develop action plans to address these gaps. Engage with stakeholders to gather diverse perspectives and ensure a holistic understanding of ethical considerations. This assessment can be a foundation for implementing ethical AI practices and building a culture of responsibility and trust.

7.1 DATA PRIVACY: PROTECTING CUSTOMER INFORMATION

In today's digital landscape, understanding key data privacy regulations is more important than ever. As an entrepreneur, navigating the complex terrain of laws like the General Data Protection Regulation (GDPR) and the California Consumer Privacy Act (CCPA) is crucial for maintaining customer trust and avoiding hefty fines. GDPR, which applies to any entity processing the data of EU residents, demands a robust approach to privacy, emphasizing 'privacy by default.' This means businesses must integrate data protection into their processes from the outset. Essential requirements include:

- Obtaining explicit consent for data collection and processing.
- Ensuring data is processed transparently
- Enabling individuals to access or delete their data upon request.

Meanwhile, CCPA focuses on enhancing transparency and consumer control for California residents. It allows consumers to know what personal data is being collected, opt out of data sales, and request the deletion of their information. Both regulations aim to protect personal data but differ in enforcement and penalties, with GDPR imposing stricter fines. Navigating these regulations effectively is not just about compliance but building trust with your customers.

Establishing robust privacy policies is not merely a regulatory requirement but a cornerstone of building and maintaining customer trust. Start by developing comprehensive data collection and retention policies that outline what data is collected, how it is used, and how long it will be stored. Clearly define the purpose of data collection, ensuring it aligns with your business objectives and complies with legal requirements. Implement customer consent mechanisms that are clear and straightforward, allowing users to opt-in to data collection knowingly. These mechanisms should provide detailed data usage information and offer users options to manage their preferences. Regularly review and update your privacy policies to reflect regulations and business practices changes, maintaining transparency and accountability. By prioritizing privacy, you demonstrate a commitment to protecting your customers' information and fostering long-term relationships based on trust and respect.

Leveraging privacy-enhancing technologies is a proactive approach to safeguarding customer data and strengthening security measures. Data anonymization techniques play a critical role here, allowing businesses to use data without compromising individual privacy. By removing or encrypting personally identifiable information, you can minimize the risk of data breaches while still deriving valuable insights from the data. Encryption methods for sensitive data at rest and in transit further enhance security by ensuring that only authorized personnel can access sensitive information. Implementing secure communication protocols, such as Transport Layer Security (TLS), helps protect data during transmission, preventing unauthorized access. Regularly audit your data systems to identify vulnerabilities and apply the latest security patches, reinforcing your defenses against potential threats. By adopting these technologies, you protect customer information and build a reputation for reliability and security in the digital age.

Educating employees on best data privacy practices is an investment that pays dividends in enhanced security and compliance. Start by conducting regular privacy training workshops that cover the latest regulations, technologies, and company policies. These workshops should be interactive and engaging, encouraging employees to ask questions and participate actively. Providing employee handbooks on data protection can serve as a valuable reference tool, outlining key responsibilities and procedures for handling data securely. Encourage a culture of vigilance, where employees understand the importance of data privacy and feel empowered to report potential issues. Regularly update training materials to reflect changes in the regulatory landscape and emerging threats, ensuring that your team is always prepared to handle data responsibly. By prioritizing education, you create a knowledgeable workforce equipped to protect customer information and uphold your company's commitment to privacy.

7.2 RISK MANAGEMENT: IDENTIFYING AND MITIGATING AI RISKS

Incorporating AI into business operations can significantly enhance efficiency, but it also introduces unique risks that must be managed proactively. Conducting comprehensive risk assessments is the first step in this process. Imagine your business as a ship navigating through unknown waters; a risk assessment serves as your map, identifying potential threats that could disrupt your course. Start using established risk assessment frameworks that provide a structured approach to evaluating potential vulnerabilities in your AI systems. These frameworks help you examine every facet of your AI applications, from data integrity to system security, ensuring nothing is overlooked. Identifying vulnerabilities requires a keen eye for detail and an understanding of how AI interacts with various elements of your business. For instance, consider how data flows through your systems and where it might be most exposed to threats. You can develop strategies to fortify your defenses and protect your business from potential disruptions by pinpointing these weak spots.

Once you've identified potential risks, developing robust risk mitigation strategies is next. The key is focusing on technological and operational measures that effectively address identified vulnerabilities. Redundancy and failover systems are crucial components of any risk mitigation strategy. These systems ensure that if one part of your AI infrastructure fails, another can seamlessly take its place, minimizing downtime and maintaining business continuity. Regular software updates and patches are equally important, as they protect your systems from new vulnerabilities and cyber threats. Keeping your AI software up-to-date ensures you are always ahead of potential risks, safeguarding your business from disruptions. Additionally, consider implementing multi-layered security measures that provide comprehensive protection against various threats. By adopting a proactive approach to risk mitigation, you can create a resilient AI infrastructure that supports your business objectives while minimizing exposure to risks.

An effective incident response plan is essential for addressing data breaches or AI failures swiftly and efficiently. Think of it as your business's emergency manual detailing the steps to take when things go wrong. Establish clear roles and responsibilities within your incident response team, ensuring that everyone knows their part in the event of a crisis. This team should include members with AI, cybersecurity, and communication expertise, each bringing valuable skills to manage incidents effectively. Communication protocols are another critical aspect of your incident response plan. These protocols outline how information should be shared during an incident, both internally and externally. Ensure your team can communicate quickly and clearly, minimizing confusion and enabling rapid response. Regularly test and update your incident response plan to reflect any changes in your AI systems or business operations, ensuring it remains effective in the face of evolving threats.

Continuous monitoring and reviewing AI risks are vital for adapting to new threats and vulnerabilities. Risk monitoring tools and dashboards provide real-time insights into your AI systems, allowing you to detect and respond to potential issues before they escalate.

These tools can track various metrics, from system performance to threat detection, providing a comprehensive view of your risk land-scape. Regular risk review meetings should be scheduled to discuss these insights, bringing together key stakeholders to evaluate current risks and adjust strategies. This ongoing process ensures that your risk management efforts remain relevant and practical, enabling you to stay ahead of potential challenges. By fostering a culture of vigilance and adaptability, you can ensure that your AI systems continue to support your business goals while minimizing exposure to risks.

7.3 BUILDING TRUST: TRANSPARENCY IN AI OPERATIONS

Imagine you're in a bustling town square, where every interaction is open and visible. Transparency in AI operates much like this, fostering trust through clear and open communication. When busi-nesses openly communicate about their AI capabilities, they demys-tify processes often hidden behind complex algorithms. This openness begins with making AI documentation publicly available. By doing so, you allow customers and stakeholders to see the inner workings of your AI systems, creating an environment where trust can flourish. This approach builds confidence and aligns with the increasing demand for transparency in technology. When stake-holders understand how AI decisions are made, they're more likely to trust the outcomes, knowing there's nothing to hide.

Communicating AI-driven decisions clearly is crucial for main-taining trust and ensuring users understand the rationale behind AI actions. Imagine receiving a letter with a decision that affects you but is filled with jargon and technicalities you need help compre-hending. It's frustrating, right? AI decisions shouldn't feel like that.

They need plain language explanations that break down complex processes into understandable terms. This clarity helps bridge the gap between technical operations and everyday understanding.

Additionally, establishing customer feedback mechanisms allows users to voice their opinions on AI outcomes, offering valuable insights for improvement. These feedback loops enhance transparency and empower customers, making them active participants in the AI ecosystem. By engaging with users, businesses can refine AI systems and ensure they meet their audience's needs and expectations.

Involving stakeholders in developing and implementing AI systems is a powerful way to build trust and ensure alignment with business goals. Stakeholder workshops serve as collaborative forums where diverse perspectives can be shared and considered. These gatherings allow stakeholders to engage directly with AI projects, offering feedback and insights that can shape the development direction. Collaborative AI development initiatives further enhance this engagement by involving stakeholders in decision-making. Businesses and stakeholders can co-create AI solutions that reflect shared values and priorities by working together. This collaborative approach strengthens trust and fosters a sense of ownership and commitment among all parties involved.

Committing to ethical AI practices can significantly enhance a business's reputation and trustworthiness. Public declarations of ethical AI commitments signal to customers and stakeholders that a business is serious about responsible AI use. These declarations can take the form of corporate social responsibility (CSR) reports, which detail the ethical standards and practices guiding AI implementation. CSR reports provide transparency into a business's ethical considerations, showcasing how AI aligns with broader social and environmental goals. By publicly committing to ethical AI practices, companies can differentiate themselves in a competitive market, building a solid reputation for integrity and responsibility. This commitment to ethics attracts customers and fosters long-term relationships based on trust and mutual respect.

As we reflect on the importance of transparency, it's evident that building trust in AI operations requires ongoing commitment and communication. Businesses can create a foundation of trust by fostering open dialogue, clearly explaining AI decisions, engaging stakeholders, and showcasing ethical obligations. This trust is essential for navigating the complexities of AI in today's digital landscape, ensuring that technology serves the greater good while empowering businesses and stakeholders alike. As we progress, these principles of transparency and trust will continue to guide our exploration of AI's potential, setting the stage for further innovation and growth.

CHAPTER 8

Industry-Specific AI Insights

I magine stepping into a retail store where the shelves anticipate your every need, offering just the right products as if they were handpicked. This isn't a scene from a futuristic movie but a reality AI is creating in today's retail industry. As an entrepreneur, you constantly seek ways to enhance customer satisfaction and loyalty. AI-driven recommendation engines are at the forefront of this transformation, analyzing customer behavior and preferences to curate personalized shopping experiences. These engines comb through purchase history, online behavior, and social media interactions to suggest products that resonate with individual tastes. This level of personalization boosts customer satisfaction and significantly increases loyalty by making consumers feel valued and understood. According to a 2018 Accenture report, 91% of consumers prefer brands that remember their preferences and offer relevant suggestions, underscoring the power of hyper-personalization in today's market.

Moreover, personalized marketing campaigns have become a game-changer for brands looking to increase conversion rates and reduce cart abandonment. By tailoring marketing efforts based on comprehensive customer profiles, businesses can engage with their audience more meaningfully. These campaigns can include targeted discounts or dynamic ads at the right moment, enticing the customer to purchase. This strategy strengthens consumer-brand relationships and optimizes user satisfaction, as evidenced by the 63% of companies that reported increased conversion rates after implementing personalization strategies. The integration of AI in this context enables businesses to create a seamless and consistent shopping experience across both online and offline channels, further enhancing brand loyalty.

Regarding inventory management, AI is an indispensable tool for reducing costs and improving efficiency. Predictive analytics plays a crucial role here, analyzing historical sales data and current market trends to accurately forecast demand. This capability allows businesses to optimize stock levels, ensuring they have the right products available at the right time, reducing excess inventory, and minimizing stock outs. This curtails unnecessary expenses and aligns with sustainability goals, an aspect essential to Gen Z shoppers who value eco-friendly practices. Real-time inventory tracking systems further enhance this process by providing up-to-date insights into stock levels, helping retailers make informed decisions about restocking and promotion strategies.

Brick-and-mortar stores are included in this digital revolution. AI technologies are revolutionizing in-store experiences, blurring the lines between the digital and physical worlds. Intelligent mirrors in fitting rooms are a prime example, allowing customers to try on clothes virtually and see how different styles and colors suit them without physically changing outfits. This enhances the shopping experience and encourages customers to try more products, potentially increasing sales. Virtual reality shopping experiences take this a step further by immersing customers in a digital environment where they can explore products in 3D, providing a novel and engaging way to shop. These innovations create an interactive and memorable shopping experience, separating forward-thinking retailers in a competitive market.

The supply chain, the backbone of retail, also benefits immensely from AI integration. AI-driven route optimization ensures deliveries are made efficiently, reducing lead times and cutting transportation costs. By analyzing factors like traffic patterns and weather conditions, AI systems can suggest the best routes for delivery trucks, ensuring timely arrival and reducing fuel consumption. Additionally, AI-powered supplier risk assessment tools provide insights into supplier reliability and potential risks, allowing retailers to make strategic decisions that strengthen their supply chain resilience. This proactive approach minimizes disruptions and ensures that products reach customers without delays, enhancing customer satisfaction and trust in the brand.

Case Study: AI-Driven Shopping Experience at Retail Giant

Consider the case of a leading retail giant that implemented AI-driven recommendation engines across its online platforms. By analyzing customer data and preferences, the company was able to offer personalized product suggestions, resulting in a 20% increase in conversion rates. Simultaneously, predictive analytics optimized inventory management, reducing stockouts by 30% and minimizing excess inventory costs. In physical stores, intelligent mirrors and virtual reality experiences captivated customers, encouraging them to explore more products and enhancing overall satisfaction. This comprehensive AI strategy boosted sales and solidified the brand's reputation as a leader in innovative retail experiences. The case demonstrates the tangible benefits of embracing AI in retail, paving the way for others to follow.

8.1 ENHANCING HEALTHCARE: AI APPLICATIONS IN MEDICINE

Healthcare is witnessing unprecedented changes, mainly due to the integration of AI, redefining how medical professionals approach diagnostics. With AI-powered image analysis, the ability to interpret X-rays and MRIs has reached new heights. This technology uses complex algorithms to scrutinize images with precision, highlighting potential issues that might be overlooked by the human eye. For instance, AI systems can detect anomalies in medical imaging, flagging areas that require further attention, thus speeding up the diagnosis process. These systems provide crucial support to radiologists, allowing them to make more accurate diagnoses and initiate timely medical interventions.

Moreover, predictive models are proving instrumental in forecasting disease outbreaks. By analyzing patterns across vast data sets, these models can anticipate the spread of infectious diseases, enabling healthcare providers to take preventive measures and allocate resources efficiently. This proactive approach saves lives and reduces the burden on healthcare systems, ensuring they can respond swiftly to emerging health threats.

Patient care and monitoring are also being transformed by AI, which offers a more personalized approach to healthcare. Wearable devices equipped with AI analytics are now commonplace, keeping track of vital signs and providing continuous health monitoring. These devices collect real-time data, analyzing heart rate, activity levels, and sleep patterns to offer personalized health insights. Such tools empower individuals to take charge of their health, providing doctors with valuable data to tailor care plans to each patient's needs. Furthermore, AI-driven telemedicine platforms are revolutionizing access to healthcare. Patients can consult with doctors remotely, receiving expert advice without traveling. This not only increases accessibility, especially for those in remote areas but also reduces strain on healthcare facilities by minimizing unnecessary visits. These platforms incorporate AI to diagnose symptoms, offering a seamless and efficient healthcare experience that bridges geographical barriers and enhances patient engagement.

Administrative tasks in healthcare have long been a source of frustration for professionals, diverting time away from patient care. However, AI is alleviating this burden by automating routine processes. Consider appointment scheduling, a task that often involves considerable time and coordination. Automated AI-powered systems can easily handle these tasks, managing appointments based on patient preferences and doctor availability while sending reminders to reduce no-shows. This streamlining allows healthcare providers to focus more on patient interactions and less on logistical challenges.

Similarly, AI-based medical record management systems organize and maintain patient data efficiently. These systems ensure that records are up-to-date and easily accessible, facilitating quick retrieval and reducing doctors' time on paperwork. By optimizing these administrative functions, AI frees healthcare professionals to concentrate on what truly matters: delivering exceptional patient care.

In drug discovery and research, AI is a catalyst for innovation, accelerating traditionally lengthy and costly processes. AI algorithms sift through massive datasets to identify potential drug candidates, analyzing chemical properties and biological effects to predict efficacy and safety. This capability significantly reduces the time required to pinpoint viable compounds, enabling researchers to focus on the most promising possibilities. Machine learning models further enhance this process by optimizing clinical trials. These models analyze patient data to match individuals with suitable trials, improving trial outcomes and streamlining the research phase. By enhancing the efficiency of drug discovery, AI reduces development costs and expedites the introduction of new treatments to the market. This advancement is pivotal in addressing global health challenges, ensuring that effective therapies reach patients faster than ever before.

Reflection Section: AI's Influence on Healthcare

Consider how AI could reshape specific aspects of healthcare practices you are familiar with. Reflect on the potential benefits and challenges of integrating AI into these areas. What steps would need to be taken to ensure successful implementation? Discuss with colleagues or peers to gain diverse perspectives and insights.

8.2 AI IN FINANCE: REDUCING RISK AND INCREASING RETURNS

In the fast-paced world of finance, AI emerges as a formidable force, particularly in fraud detection and prevention. Imagine a bustling financial institution processing millions of transactions each day. Hidden within this vast sea of data are anomalies—subtle patterns that could signal fraudulent activity. AI excels at detecting these anomalies by meticulously analyzing transaction patterns and identifying irregularities that might escape human scrutiny. This capability is crucial for banks and financial institutions striving to protect their assets and maintain customer trust. AI-powered systems offer real-time fraud alerts, enabling swift responses to suspicious activities. These systems continuously monitor transactions, learning and adapting to new fraud techniques, which ensures they remain effective in the face of evolving threats. This proactive approach minimizes financial losses and enhances the institution's reputation for security and reliability.

Thanks to AI's ability to analyze market data with unprecedented depth, investment strategies have also transformed. In the world of stock markets, information is power. AI-driven portfolio management tools allow investors to harness this power by processing vast market data to identify trends and opportunities. These tools use complex algorithms to forecast market movements, helping investors make informed decisions. Sentiment analysis, another innovative application, scans news articles, social media chatter, and financial reports to gauge market sentiment. By understanding the emotional tone of the market, investors can anticipate shifts and adjust their strategies accordingly. This blend of data-driven insights and emotional intelligence gives investors a competitive edge, allowing them to optimize their portfolios for maximum returns. AI's role in investment strategy is a testament to its potential to revolutionize financial decision-making, turning data into actionable insights that drive profitability.

The banking sector is no stranger to AI's transformative power, particularly in enhancing customer experiences. Picture a customer interacting with a bank's app, seeking assistance with account queries or financial advice. AI-driven chatbots step in, offering instant, around-the-clock support. These chatbots are designed to handle routine inquiries, giving customers quick and accurate responses. They are efficient and personable, mimicking human conversation to create a seamless interaction. Beyond customer service, AI personalizes banking experiences by analyzing spending habits to offer tailored financial advice. This might include suggesting savings plans, optimizing credit card usage, or providing alerts on unusual spending. Such personalization enhances customer satisfaction, as clients receive relevant and valuable services for their financial goals. In a world where customer expectations are continually rising, AI ensures banks can meet and exceed these demands, fostering loyalty and trust.

Risk management in finance has always been critical, and AI is revolutionizing how financial institutions assess and manage these risks. Traditional credit-scoring models often rely on static data, which can be limiting. AI, however, leverages machine learning to develop dynamic credit scoring models that consider a broader range of factors. These models continuously learn from new data, more accurately assessing a borrower's creditworthiness. This improves loan approval processes and reduces the risk of defaults. Predictive analytics further enhance risk management by analyzing historical data to forecast potential risks, such as market volatility or economic downturns. By identifying these risks early, financial institutions can implement strategies to mitigate them, safeguarding their assets and ensuring stability. AI'sapplication in risk manage- ment exemplifies its ability to provide financial institutions with the tools needed to confidently navigate uncertainty.

8.3 MANUFACTURING AND AI: AUTOMATING PRODUCTION PROCESSES

Imagine a sprawling factory floor, bustling with the hum of machinery yet running smoother than ever before. This is the reality AI is crafting in the manufacturing industry. Machines no longer wait until something goes wrong to be fixed; AI-driven predictive maintenance ensures they stay in top working condition. By analyzing data from sensors embedded in equipment, AI systems can forecast potential failures before they occur, scheduling maintenance precisely when needed. This approach minimizes downtime and extends the machinery's lifespan, saving costs and enhancing productivity.

Similarly, quality control has taken a leap forward with AI's integration. Using computer vision, AI systems inspect products exceptionally, identifying defects that might slip past human inspectors. This ensures that only top-quality products leave the factory, reducing waste and returns and ultimately protecting brand reputation.

The concept of smart manufacturing, often called Industry 4.0, is becoming a reality, primarily due to AI's ability to coordinate complex processes seamlessly. These smart factories are characterized by IoT integration, where sensors and devices communicate, sharing real-time data. This connectivity allows for a comprehensive overview of operations, enabling managers to make informed decisions quickly. AI plays a vital role here, analyzing the data to optimize production schedules, resource allocation, and energy consumption. Autonomous robotic systems are at the heart of these intelligent factories, working alongside human employees to enhance efficiency. These robots precisely handle repetitive tasks, freeing human workers to focus on more strategic activities. The synergy between AI and robotics boosts productivity and creates a safer working environment as robots take on tasks that might pose risks to human health.

AI is a game-changer in the intricate world of supply chains, where even a minor disruption can have significant repercussions. By employing sophisticated algorithms for demand forecasting, AI helps manufacturers anticipate market needs with uncanny accuracy. This foresight allows them to adjust production levels proactively, reducing the risk of overproduction or stockouts. Additionally, AI enhances supplier optimization and risk management, evaluating the reliability and performance of suppliers to mitigate potential disruptions. This comprehensive approach to supply chain management ensures that manufacturers can maintain a steady flow of materials and products, even in the face of unexpected challenges. AI's resilience to supply chains is invaluable, enabling manufacturers to adapt swiftly to changing market conditions and customer demands.

Sustainability is no longer a buzzword but a necessity, and AI is helping manufacturers align their operations with eco-friendly practices. AI systems optimize energy consumption by analyzing patterns and identifying areas where efficiency can be improved. This reduces energy use and lower emissions, contributing to a smaller carbon footprint. Moreover, AI-driven process improvements target waste reduction, identifying ways to minimize scrap and optimize material use. These sustainable practices lower operational costs and appeal to consumers increasingly conscious of environmental impact. By embracing AI, manufacturers can balance profitability and sustainability, ensuring long-term success in a competitive market.

As we conclude this chapter, integrating AI into manufacturing processes emerges as a transformative force, driving efficiency, resilience, and sustainability. The marriage of technology and manufacturing sets new standards, pushing industries toward more innovative, adaptive, and environmentally friendly practices. As we move forward, the next chapter will explore how AI continues to expand its influence, shaping industries and redefining possibilities.

CHAPTER 9

Future Trends and Innovations in AI

I n the dim glow of a bustling conference hall, an engineer
unveils a breakthrough that promises to redefine the boundaries
of innovation—quantum computing intertwined with artificial intelligence. This revelation sparks a buzz among entrepreneurs and tech
enthusiasts alike, hinting at a future where the limits of computational power are shattered and new possibilities emerge. Quantum
computing, an area that has captivated significant tech players like
IBM and Google, introduces a paradigm shift from traditional
computing. Unlike classical bits, quantum bits, or cubits, can exist
in multiple states simultaneously, allowing exponentially faster and
more complex computations. For entrepreneurs, this means the
potential to solve problems previously deemed impossible, such as
optimizing intricate logistics networks or accelerating drug
discovery processes. Quantum machine learning, a subfield poised
to revolutionize AI, leverages these capabilities to enhance data
processing speed and efficiency, promising more sophisticated AI
models. While still in its nascent stages, the fusion of quantum

computing and AI beckons a future where businesses can harness unimaginable computational power to drive innovation and growth.

As we chart the future of AI, edge computing emerges as a pivotal force in enhancing efficiency and security. In contrast to traditional cloud computing, edge computing processes data at the source, reducing latency and ensuring real-time decision-making. This shift is particularly transformative for Internet of Things (IoT) devices, which require immediate responses to data inputs. Imagine a network of intelligent traffic lights in a bustling city, each equipped with AI to manage traffic flow based on real-time conditions. These systems can instantly adapt to changing traffic patterns by processing data locally, minimizing congestion, and improving urban mobility. Edge AI also bolsters data privacy by limiting the transmission of sensitive information to centralized servers, a critical consideration for industries where data security is paramount. As smart cities evolve, edge computing stands at the forefront, offering a blueprint for responsive, efficient, and secure urban environments.

Autonomous systems, another frontier in AI, are steadily gaining traction across various sectors, promising to reshape how we interact with technology. From autonomous vehicles navigating complex urban landscapes to drones delivering essential supplies to remote areas, these systems are powered by advanced AI algorithms that enable them to operate independently with minimal human intervention. Although in its early stages, autonomous vehicle technology holds the promise of transforming transportation by enhancing safety and reducing traffic congestion. Meanwhile, AI-controlled delivery drones are revolutionizing logistics by providing rapid and efficient delivery solutions, particularly in areas with limited infrastructure. These advancements improve operational efficiency and open new avenues for businesses to explore innovative delivery models, catering to the growing demand for swift and reliable services. As these technologies mature, they present opportunities for entrepreneurs to capitalize on the shift towards automation, offering services that redefine convenience and accessibility.

Amidst these technological advancements, the focus on AI ethics and governance is becoming increasingly important. As AI systems become more integrated into daily life, ensuring their ethical development and use is crucial to maintaining public trust and fostering innovation. AI governance frameworks like the OECD AI Principles and the EU AI Act provide guidelines to address issues like bias, privacy, and transparency. These frameworks emphasize the need for accountability and fairness, ensuring AI systems respect human rights and operate transparently. For entrepreneurs, understanding and implementing these guidelines is essential for building trustworthy AI solutions that align with societal values. Engaging with AI ethics boards and adhering to regulatory standards can mitigate risks associated with AI deployment, safeguarding against potential misuse or unintended consequences. As the AI landscape evolves, navigating the intersection of technology and ethics will be critical to unlocking its full potential while ensuring its benefits are accessible and equitable.

Reflection Section: Navigating Emerging AI Technologies

Consider how your business might integrate these emerging AI technologies. Reflect on the potential impact of quantum computing, edge computing, and autonomous systems on your operations. What ethical considerations might you need to address as you adopt these innovations? Use this reflection to develop a strategy that balances technological advancement with moral responsibility, ensuring your business is poised to thrive in an evolving digital landscape.

9.1 THE ROLE OF AI IN SUSTAINABILITY: GREEN INNOVATIONS

As you look to the future of your business, consider how artificial intelligence could play a pivotal role in achieving sustainability goals. One of AI's most promising applications lies in energy efficiency. Imagine a world where energy usage is finely tuned to meet needs without waste, thanks to AI-driven energy management systems. These systems optimize energy consumption across various sectors by predicting demand and adapting in real time. For example, AI can adjust lighting and heating in office buildings based on occupancy and weather forecasts, significantly reducing energy waste. Innovative grid technology further enhances this by balancing supply and demand dynamically, integrating renewable energy sources like solar and wind more effectively. As energy costs rise and environmental concerns grow, investing in AI for energy management offers financial savings and a reduced carbon footprint, presenting a compelling opportunity for businesses eager to lead in sustainability.

Beyond energy management, AI is proving instrumental in environmental monitoring and preservation. Across the globe, AI algorithms aid scientists in tracking wildlife populations and assessing the health of natural habitats. These algorithms process data from drones and satellite imagery, identifying patterns and changes that might go unnoticed. For instance, AI can detect illegal deforestation activities by analyzing satellite data, enabling authorities to respond swiftly to protect endangered ecosystems. Moreover, environmental impact assessments benefit from AI's analytical power, providing insights into air and water quality, soil health, and biodiversity. By leveraging AI, businesses can ensure that their operations comply with environmental regulations and contribute positively to climate change mitigation efforts. This proactive approach safeguards the planet and enhances brand reputation, appealing to eco-conscious consumers and stakeholders.

AI is driving a revolution towards more sustainable practices and bolstering food security in agriculture. Powered by AI sensors, precision agriculture allows farmers to monitor crop health and soil conditions with unprecedented accuracy. These sensors collect data on moisture levels, nutrient content, and pest activity, enabling farmers to apply resources like water and fertilizers more efficiently. This targeted approach reduces waste and environmental impact while improving crop yields. Additionally, AI-driven crop yield optimization tools analyze weather patterns and historical data to predict optimal planting and harvesting times. By maximizing output and minimizing resource use, these innovations support sustainable farming practices crucial in feeding a growing global population. As you explore AI's potential in agriculture, consider how these technologies could enhance your operations, leading to greater efficiency and sustainability.

The concept of a circular economy, where waste is minimized and resources are continually reused, is gaining traction, with AI playing a significant role in this transition. AI-driven recycling and waste management systems can sort and process materials more effectively, improving the quality and efficiency of recycling processes. For instance, AI-powered machines can identify and separate different types of plastics, metals, and paper, reducing contamination and increasing the value of recycled materials. Moreover, product lifecycle analysis through AI provides insights into the environmental impact of products from creation to disposal.

Such analyses can guide businesses in designing more sustainable products and choosing materials that are easier to recycle or have a lower carbon footprint. By embracing AI, companies can support a circular economy model that conserves resources and offers new opportunities for innovation and growth. As you consider this approach, consider how AI can help align your business practices with sustainability principles, creating value for both the environment and your bottom line.

9.2 AI AND THE GIG ECONOMY: NEW OPPORTUNITIES FOR ENTREPRENEURS

In the evolving landscape of the gig economy, AI is emerging as a powerful ally for both platforms and workers. Imagine a bustling online marketplace where AI-powered algorithms match gig workers with jobs that perfectly align with their skills, preferences, and availability. These advanced matching engines analyze vast amounts of data to ensure that every gig worker is paired with tasks that fit their unique strengths, optimizing job satisfaction and productivity. Personalized recommendations further enhance the user experience, allowing gig workers to receive tailored suggestions for opportunities that align with their career goals. This level of customization improves job matching and enhances the overall user experience, making gig platforms more efficient and attractive to job seekers and employers.

AI also transforms skill development within the gig economy, offering tools that facilitate continuous learning and growth. Picture AI-driven training platforms that provide gig workers personalized learning paths to upskill or reskill in their chosen fields. These platforms leverage AI to assess individual learning styles and progress, offering customized content that addresses specific knowledge gaps.

Virtual mentors, powered by AI, provide guidance and feedback, simulating real-world interactions with seasoned professionals. This approach democratizes education, allowing gig workers to enhance their skills at their own pace and convenience. As the gig economy expands, these AI-driven tools play a crucial role in equipping workers with the competencies needed to thrive in a competitive market.

The rise of AI has also spurred new opportunities within the gig economy, particularly in remote work facilitation. With AI-enhanced collaboration tools, gig workers can connect with clients and colleagues across the globe, transcending geographical boundaries. These tools offer real-time language translation, seamless document sharing, and virtual meeting spaces, making remote teamwork more efficient and effective. Additionally, AI development itself presents a burgeoning field for freelancers. As businesses increasingly seek AI expertise, freelance opportunities in AI programming, data analysis, and model training are rising. This growing demand provides gig workers new avenues to explore, offering diverse and lucrative career paths in the digital age.

Despite the numerous opportunities, gig workers often face income stability and job security challenges. Here, AI can offer solutions to mitigate these issues. Financial planning tools driven by AI help gig workers manage their earnings, forecast potential income, and plan for taxes and expenses. These tools analyze patterns in gig work income, providing insights that enable workers to budget effectively and maintain financial stability. AI-driven benefits management platforms also play a pivotal role, offering gig workers access to benefits typically reserved for full-time employees, such as health insurance and retirement savings plans. By automating benefits administration and personalizing options based on individual needs, these platforms ensure that gig workers receive the support they need to succeed.

Interactive Element: Gig Economy AI Toolkit

Consider exploring an AI toolkit explicitly designed for the gig economy. This resource can include links to AI-powered job-matching platforms, personalized learning apps for skill development, and financial management tools tailored to gig workers' needs. By leveraging these resources, gig workers can optimize their experience, enhance their skills, and secure their financial future. This toolkit empowers workers and encourages innovation and adaptability within the gig economy, setting the stage for ongoing growth and success.

Integrating AI into the gig economy is transforming how work is done and reshaping the very nature of employment. As AI advances, it brings a wealth of opportunities and challenges that demand attention. Understanding and leveraging these developments is critical for entrepreneurs to stay competitive and innovative. The gig economy, fueled by AI advancements, is poised to become a dynamic and integral part of the modern workforce, offering flexibility and efficiency in an increasingly digital and interconnected world.

9.3 PREPARING FOR CHANGE: ADAPTING TO AI-DRIVEN MARKET SHIFTS

In the rapidly evolving landscape of AI, fostering a culture of innovation isn't just beneficial—it's necessary. Businesses must embrace a mindset that continuously seeks improvement and adaptation. This involves creating spaces where creativity and experimentation thrive, such as innovation labs. These labs provide a playground for testing new AI solutions, allowing teams to iterate and refine ideas in a low-risk environment. Cross-functional innovation teams, composed of members from diverse departments, can further enhance this process. By bringing together varied perspectives, these teams can tackle challenges more creatively and develop solutions that might not emerge in a siloed setting. Encouraging such collaboration sparks innovation and builds a resilient organizational culture capable of facing the challenges of an AI-driven market head-on.

As AI technologies evolve, so must the skills of the workforce. Continuous learning becomes a cornerstone for success, ensuring employees remain updated with the latest advancements and industry demands. Businesses can invest in AI-focused learning and development programs, providing staff with the necessary resources to thrive. These programs might include workshops, webinars, or even immersive courses that delve into the intricacies of AI technology and its applications. Partnering with educational institutions can further enrich these learning opportunities, offering access to cutting-edge research and expertise. By prioritizing education and skill development, businesses enhance their competitive edge and empower their workforce, fostering a culture of growth and adaptability.

Implementing effective change management strategies is crucial as AI reshapes organizational landscapes. These strategies provide a structured approach to managing transitions, ensuring that changes are integrated smoothly and effectively. Developing change management frameworks can help guide organizations through the complexities of AI adoption, addressing potential resistance and aligning new technologies with existing processes. Employee engagement initiatives during these transitions are equally important, as they cultivate a sense of ownership and involvement. By actively involving employees in the change process, businesses can mitigate anxiety and foster a supportive environment where innovation thrives. This proactive approach facilitates smoother transitions and strengthens the organization's foundation for growth.

Anticipating market disruptions is integral to strategic planning in an AI-driven world. Businesses must be prepared to adapt to rapid technological shifts that redefine industries overnight. Scenario planning can be a powerful tool in this regard, allowing organizations to explore various future scenarios and develop strategies to respond effectively. Businesses can identify opportunities and threats by considering potential outcomes and crafting flexible plans that accommodate changing circumstances. In tandem with scenario planning, risk management strategies help organizations navigate the uncertainties associated with technological advancements. By assessing potential risks and developing mitigation plans, businesses can Csafeguard against disruptions and position themselves to capitalize on emerging opportunities. This forward-thinking approach ensures resilience and positions businesses as leaders in the ever-evolving AI landscape.

As we look to the future, embracing change and innovation becomes central to thriving in an AI-driven market. By fostering a culture of creativity, investing in continuous learning, implementing effective change management, and anticipating disruptions, businesses can confidently navigate modern technology's complexities. This chapter underscores the importance of adaptability in rapid technological advancements, setting the stage for leaders to inspire and guide their teams through the exciting opportunities AI brings.

CHAPTER 10

Building an AI-Driven Company Culture

I magine walking into a bustling workspace where innovation is palpable, and ideas flow as freely as the morning coffee. The air is charged with the excitement of a team united in a shared vision—leveraging the transformative power of AI to drive the company forward. This isn't a scene from a tech startup in Silicon Valley but a reality that any business can achieve with exemplary leadership and a cultural foundation. As AI reshapes the business landscape, leadership becomes crucial in guiding organizations through this transformative period. Leadership in the age of AI is about more than just adopting new technologies; it's about cultivating a culture that embraces change, encourages innovation, and aligns with a visionary outlook.

Cultivating a visionary leadership style is pivotal in navigating the AI landscape. Leaders must craft a clear and compelling vision that integrates AI into the organization's core mission. This vision should articulate the potential benefits of AI and inspire teams to align their efforts toward these goals. Vision statements incorporating AI goals act as guiding lights, providing direction and purpose. Leadership workshops on AI trends can further equip leaders with the knowledge and tools to drive this vision forward. By staying informed about the latest developments in AI, leaders can make informed decisions that position their companies at the forefront of innovation. These workshops allow leaders to exchange ideas, learn from industry experts, and refine their strategic approach to AI integration.

In the rapidly evolving world of AI, embracing adaptability in leadership is essential. Leaders must be prepared to navigate the fast-paced changes that AI technologies bring. This requires a mindset open to change and ready to pivot strategies as needed. Adaptive leadership training programs can equip leaders with the skills to manage uncertainty and effectively lead their teams through transitions. These programs focus on building resilience, fostering a culture of continuous learning, and encouraging experimentation. Scenario planning for AI disruptions is another critical tool for leaders. By anticipating potential challenges and opportunities, leaders can develop contingency plans that ensure their organizations remain agile and responsive. This proactive approach mitigates risks and positions companies to capitalize on emerging trends and technologies.

Modeling AI-driven decision-making is a hallmark of effective leadership in the AI era. Leaders must leverage data and insights generated by AI to make informed decisions that drive business success. AI-driven strategic planning sessions allow leaders to analyze data trends, identify opportunities, and develop actionable strategies. Real-time data dashboards provide executives with a comprehensive view of business performance, enabling them to make timely and informed decisions. Leaders can inspire their teams to embrace a similar approach by setting an example of data-driven decision-making. This creates a culture where decisions are based on evidence and insights rather than intuition alone. As a result, organizations become more efficient, innovative, and competitive in the marketplace.

Fostering a culture of trust and empowerment is crucial for leaders looking to harness the full potential of AI. Leaders must create an environment where employees feel empowered to experiment, innovate, and contribute to AI initiatives. Open-door policies for innovation proposals encourage employees to share ideas and collaborate on projects. Recognition programs for AI-driven success celebrate achievements and reinforce the value of innovation within the organization. By recognizing and rewarding employees for their contributions, leaders can motivate teams to continue pushing the boundaries of what's possible with AI. This culture of trust and empowerment drives innovation and fosters a sense of ownership and engagement among employees. As leaders build this culture, they lay the foundation for sustainable growth and long-term success.

Interactive Element: Vision Statement Workshop

Consider organizing a vision statement workshop to engage your team in shaping the company's AI goals. Encourage participants to brainstorm ideas, share insights, and collaborate on crafting a vision that resonates with the entire organization. This exercise fosters alignment, encourages buy-in, and ensures that the vision reflects the collective aspirations of the team. Leaders can build a sense of ownership and commitment by involving employees in the vision-setting process, driving the organization toward its AI-driven future with purpose and determination.

10.1 EMPLOYEE ENGAGEMENT: ENCOURAGING AI ADOPTION

Imagine walking through a workspace buzzing with energy, where employees are aware of AI's potential and eager to engage with it. This environment stems from an AI awareness and understanding foundation cultivated through strategic initiatives. AI onboarding sessions for new hires set the stage, introducing them to the company's AI tools and applications. These sessions demystify AI, breaking down complex concepts into digestible pieces. It's not just the new employees who benefit; company-wide AI newsletters keep everyone informed, sharing success stories and updates on the latest AI developments. This continuous flow of information creates a culture of curiosity and openness, where employees feel empowered to explore AI's possibilities and contribute to its integration.

Creating incentives that inspire employees to embrace and utilize AI tools is essential to encourage AI adoption. Designing programs that reward innovative use of AI can be a game-changer. Consider setting up AI adoption competitions where teams or individuals showcase how they've used AI to improve processes or solve challenges. Rewarding the most impactful projects fosters a competitive spirit and promotes creative thinking. Recognition for AI-enhanced performance, whether through bonuses or public acknowledgment, further motivates employees to integrate AI into their daily tasks. Organizations can accelerate the integration process by aligning incentives with AI adoption, making AI a natural part of the workflow rather than an imposed requirement.

Open communication channels are vital in addressing employee concerns and gathering feedback on AI initiatives. Regular AI town hall meetings provide a platform for discussion, allowing employees to voice their questions and ideas. These gatherings create a sense of community where everyone feels heard and valued. Feedback loops are equally important, offering a structured way for employees to share their experiences with AI tools. This feedback is invaluable, guiding improvements and ensuring that AI solutions meet the workforce's needs. By fostering an environment where communication flows freely, organizations can overcome resistance to change and build a supportive network that champions AI adoption.

Engagement reaches its peak when employees are actively involved in AI development. Encouraging participation in AI projects allows employees to contribute their unique insights and ideas, enhancing the overall effectiveness of AI solutions. Cross-departmental AI task forces can be established, bringing together diverse perspectives to tackle specific challenges. These teams foster collaboration, breaking down silos and promoting a culture of shared learning. Hackathons for employee-driven AI projects provide an exciting avenue for exploration and experimentation. These events encourage employees to explore unconventional solutions and develop innovative solutions that can be implemented company-wide. By involving employees in AI development, organizations tap into a wealth of creativity and strengthen the connection between AI initiatives and business objectives.

10.2 COLLABORATIVE INNOVATION: HARNESSING AI FOR TEAM SUCCESS

Within the vibrant ecosystem of a business committed to innovation, collaboration becomes the cornerstone of success. Encouraging cross-functional collaboration is vital to leveraging diverse expertise in AI projects. Organizations can tap into a wealth of knowledge and perspectives by assembling interdisciplinary AI project teams. These teams, comprising members from various departments, bring unique insights that enrich AI solutions. For example, a marketing expert might provide customer-centric viewpoints, while a data scientist contributes technical prowess. Fusing these perspectives fosters creativity, leading to innovative AI applications that might otherwise go unexplored.

Moreover, collaboration tools designed for remote teams can bridge geographical gaps, ensuring seamless communication and data sharing. Platforms like Slack or Microsoft Teams enable real-time interactions, making it easier for teams to collaborate effectively, regardless of location. These tools enhance productivity and ensure that AI projects benefit from continuous ideas and feedback, ultimately leading to superior outcomes.

AI has become an invaluable ally in enhancing team dynamics and productivity in the modern workplace. AI-powered collaborative platforms facilitate communication, enabling teams to work together more efficiently. These platforms integrate AI to automate routine tasks, such as scheduling meetings or organizing project timelines, freeing valuable time for creative problem-solving. Real-time team performance analytics provide managers with insights into team dynamics, helping identify areas for improvement and celebrate successes. AI offers actionable insights that enhance team effectiveness by analyzing communication patterns, workload distribution, and project progress. This data-driven approach boosts productivity and fosters a culture of transparency and accountability. When team members see the tangible impact of their efforts, motivation and engagement naturally increase, creating a positive feedback loop that drives continuous improvement.

Encouraging experimentation and risk-taking is another crucial aspect of fostering an innovative culture. Organizations must create environments where teams feel comfortable testing new ideas and taking calculated risks. Innovation labs serve as incubators for prototyping AI solutions, providing a safe space for exploration and experimentation. These labs allow teams to pilot new concepts, learn from failures, and iterate on their ideas without fearing immediate repercussions. Embracing a fail-fast approach to AI experimentation encourages teams to learn quickly, adapt, and refine their strategies. This mindset accelerates innovation and builds resilience as teams become adept at navigating the challenges and uncertainties inherent in AI projects. By promoting a culture of experimentation, organizations empower their teams to push boundaries and discover novel solutions that drive business growth.

Aligning AI projects with business goals ensures that collaborative initiatives contribute meaningfully to the organization's success. Goal alignment workshops for AI teams help clarify objectives and establish a shared understanding of how AI projects fit into the broader business strategy. These workshops facilitate open discussions, enabling teams to align their efforts with the company's mission and priorities. By developing strategic roadmaps for AI projects, teams can chart a clear path from concept to implementation, identifying key milestones and success metrics. This alignment ensures that AI projects are relevant and impactful and fosters a sense of purpose and direction among team members. When teams understand the strategic importance of their work, they are more likely to be motivated and committed to achieving excellence.

10.3 CONTINUOUS LEARNING: STAYING AHEAD IN THE AI RACE

In the ever-shifting landscape of technology, the capacity to learn and adapt quickly is invaluable. Fostering a learning-first culture is paramount to stay ahead in the AI race. This means prioritizing continuous education at all levels of the organization, ensuring that everyone, from entry-level employees to top executives, remains informed about the latest AI advancements. One way to achieve this is by developing AI learning paths tailored to different roles within the company. These paths guide employees through the necessary skills and knowledge to excel in their positions. You empower your team to take charge of their development by providing precise and structured learning opportunities.

Allocating learning and development budgets specifically for AI courses is another critical step. Investing in your employees' education enhances their skills and demonstrates your commitment to their growth and the company's long-term success. Consider offering access to reputable online AI learning platforms that provide courses from introductory to advanced levels. These platforms, such as Coursera or Udacity, often feature courses designed by industry experts and renowned institutions, ensuring high-quality content. Additionally, establishing partnerships with universities for AI workshops can offer more hands-on and immersive learning experiences. These collaborations can allow employees to learn from leading academics and practitioners in the field, further enriching their understanding and expertise.

The organization must encourage knowledge-sharing and mentorship to cultivate a thriving learning ecosystem. Establishing internal AI knowledge-sharing forums creates a space where employees can exchange insights, discuss challenges, and collaborate on solutions. Whether in person or virtual, these forums can become a hub of innovation and creativity, driving collective growth. Mentorship programs are equally crucial in distributing AI expertise throughout the company. Pairing experienced AI professionals with novices fosters an environment of guidance and support. Mentors can offer valuable advice, share their experiences, and help mentees navigate the complexities of AI integration. This accelerates learning, strengthens relationships, and builds a more cohesive and capable team.

Recognizing and celebrating learning achievements is a powerful way to motivate employees and reinforce the importance of continuous education. Implement systems to track learning progress and accomplishments through a learning achievement dashboard. This tool provides a visual representation of individual and team learning milestones, highlighting progress and identifying areas for improvement. Organizing AI certification recognition events is another way to celebrate success. These events acknowledge employees who have completed AI courses or certifications, offering them a platform to share their experiences and inspire others. Public recognition boosts morale and encourages others to pursue their learning paths, contributing to a culture of excellence and aspiration.

As you continue to build an AI-driven company culture, remember that the journey is ongoing. Staying ahead in the AI race requires dedication, curiosity, and a willingness to learn and adapt. You create an environment where innovation thrives by fostering a learning-first culture, providing access to educational resources, encouraging knowledge sharing, and celebrating achievements. This positions your organization for success in the AI era and empowers your employees to grow, contribute, and lead confidently. As we move forward, we will explore how these foundational elements of culture and education support the strategic implementation of AI across various business functions.

CHAPTER 11

Creating a Community of AI Enthusiasts

P icture yourself stepping into a bustling conference hall, the air buzzing with excitement, and the hum of conversations swirling around you. You're surrounded by passionate individuals, all eager to share their insights and learn from one another about the latest advancements in artificial intelligence. This is not just a meeting of minds but a vibrant community, a space where ideas flourish and collaborations are born. Building a network of like-minded enthusiasts in today's rapidly evolving AI landscape is more than just beneficial—it's essential. As an entrepreneur, connecting with others who share your interests can open doors to new opportunities, partnerships, and innovations that propel your business forward.

Networking in the AI community begins with identifying opportunities to connect with others who share your passion. Attending AI-focused conferences and expos is a fantastic way to immerse yourself in this dynamic field. These events bring together experts from around the globe, offering a wealth of knowledge and the chance to experience the latest AI innovations firsthand. Local AI meetups and workshops provide a more intimate setting for exchanging ideas and fostering relationships. These gatherings often focus on specific topics, allowing you to delve deeper into areas that align with your business interests. By participating in these events, you gain insights into emerging trends and position yourself within a network of professionals who can offer support, advice, and potential collaboration.

Developing practical networking skills is crucial for making the most of these opportunities. One key aspect of successful networking is crafting a compelling elevator pitch for your AI projects. This short, persuasive speech can pique interest and spark conversations, providing a foundation for more in-depth engagement. Active listening is equally essential, as well as demonstrating genuine interest in others' ideas and fostering meaningful dialogue. Engaging with others through thoughtful questions and comments can help build rapport and establish a connection beyond a simple exchange of business cards. By focusing on relationship-building and knowledge exchange, you create a network of contacts who are valuable resources and potential collaborators and supporters.

Joining professional networks dedicated to AI further solidifies your place within the community. Membership in AI professional associations offers access to exclusive resources, events, and forums where you can connect with industry leaders and peers. Additionally, participating in AI-related LinkedIn groups provides a platform for sharing insights, discussing challenges, and staying updated on the latest developments. These networks are vital for keeping your finger on the pulse of the AI industry, allowing you to stay informed and engaged in ongoing conversations. By actively participating in these networks, you demonstrate your commitment to the field and enhance your credibility as an AI enthusiast.

Fostering long-term relationships is the cornerstone of successful networking. Regular follow-ups with AI connections help maintain and strengthen these relationships, keeping the lines of communication open. Small gestures can have a significant impact, whether it's a quick email to share an interesting article or a congratulatory message on a recent achievement. Inviting contacts for coffee meetings or informal gatherings provides an opportunity for deeper discussions and collaboration. These interactions strengthen connections and create a foundation for future partnerships and mentorships. By investing time and effort into cultivating these relationships, you lay the groundwork for a supportive community that can offer guidance, inspiration, and opportunities for growth.

Interactive Element: Networking Action Plan

Consider creating a Networking Action Plan to help you navigate the world of AI networking. Start by listing upcoming AI events, conferences, and meetups you plan to attend. Next, identify key individuals or organizations you want to connect with and develop personalized strategies for reaching out to them. Finally, set goals for how many new contacts you aim to make and follow up with after each event. This proactive approach ensures you maximize your networking efforts and build a robust community of AI enthusiasts.

11.1 LEVERAGING ONLINE PLATFORMS: FORUMS AND SOCIAL MEDIA FOR AI

Imagine settling into your favorite chair after a long day, laptop open, ready to explore the expansive universe of AI online. Engaging in AI communities on the internet offers a unique opportunity to connect with enthusiasts and experts across the globe, providing a rich tapestry of ideas and insights. One of the most vibrant hubs for AI discussions is Reddit's AI Subreddits. Here, you can find everything from technical deep dives to philosophical debates on AI ethics. Participating in these forums allows you to share your perspectives and gain feedback and keeps you informed about the latest developments and challenges in the field. Similarly, AI-focused discussion boards are treasure troves of knowledge where you can pose questions, share experiences, and learn from others navigating similar paths. These platforms foster a sense of camaraderie and collective learning, essential for anyone looking to deepen their understanding of AI.

Social media has evolved into a powerful tool for collaboration, connecting you with AI professionals and enthusiasts worldwide. With its real-time updates and diverse user base, Twitter offers a unique platform for sharing and discovering AI innovations. You can stay up-to-date on breakthroughs and emerging trends by following industry leaders and engaging in Twitter threads. Conversely, LinkedIn provides a more professional setting for sharing detailed AI case studies and articles. It allows you to engage with thought leaders and peers, offering a platform for in-depth discussions and networking. Both platforms serve as conduits for knowledge exchange, enabling you to broadcast your insights and learn from the shared experiences of others. This digital landscape provides access to a wealth of information and helps you build a personal brand as an AI thought leader, expanding your influence and reach.

The digital age has democratized information sharing, allowing anyone with an internet connection to contribute to the global knowledge pool. You can educate others by sharing AI tutorials on platforms like YouTube while establishing your expertise. These tutorials can range from beginner guides to advanced courses, catering to a broad audience and enhancing your credibility in the field. Meanwhile, ResearchGate offers a dedicated space to share AI research papers and facilitate academic exchange and collaboration. By contributing to these platforms, you disseminate valuable knowledge and engage in a reciprocal learning process, receiving feedback and insights from a diverse audience. This collaborative environment encourages innovation and fosters a culture of continuous improvement, driving personal and collective growth within the AI community.

Keeping up with the rapid pace of AI advancements requires vigilance and a proactive approach. Online platforms are invaluable tools for monitoring trends and innovations in real-time. Following AI thought leaders on social media provides a direct line to expert opinions and insights, helping you anticipate shifts in the industry. Engaging in webinars and online workshops further enriches your understanding, offering interactive learning experiences led by industry pioneers. These events often cover cutting-edge topics and provide opportunities for live Q&A sessions, allowing you to delve deeper into areas of interest. By staying connected through these platforms, you ensure that your knowledge remains current and comprehensive, equipping you with the tools to navigate the ever-evolving AI landscape. This ongoing engagement enhances your expertise and positions you at the forefront of AI innovation, ready to seize emerging opportunities and tackle new challenges.

Visual Element: Online Community Map

Consider creating an online community map to maximize your online engagement with AI. This visual representation can help you track the platforms, forums, and social media groups you are involved in. Categorize each by the type of content or connections it offers and note any upcoming events or discussions of interest. This organized approach ensures you stay active across various channels, enhancing your presence and influence within the AI community.

11.2 COLLABORATIVE VENTURES: PARTNERING FOR AI SUCCESS

In the dynamic realm of AI, identifying strategic partnership opportunities can be a game-changer. Collaborations with tech startups are particularly valuable. These startups often bring fresh, innovative ideas and agile methodologies that can complement your AI initiatives. By partnering with these nimble entities, you can tap into cutting-edge technologies and creative problem-solving approaches that might be challenging to develop in-house. Consider forming alliances with startups that align with your vision and goals; their expertise can accelerate your projects and offer insights into emerging trends.

Additionally, partnerships with academic institutions present another promising avenue. Universities and research centers are at the forefront of AI advancements, offering access to groundbreaking research and a talent pool of budding AI experts. Engaging with academia enriches your knowledge base and opens doors to collaborative research projects that can drive innovation and development in your AI endeavors.

Creating win-win partnerships is the cornerstone of successful collaborations in the AI space. When structuring these partnerships, focus on mutual benefits that drive success for all parties involved. Joint ventures on AI product development are an excellent way to pool resources, expertise, and market reach. By working together, you can develop AI solutions that are not only innovative but also commercially viable. In these joint ventures, ensure that each partner's contributions and responsibilities are clearly defined to foster a sense of ownership and commitment. Shared research projects and funding can further enhance collaboration by leveraging the strengths of each partner. This approach allows you to share costs, risks, and rewards, making ambitious projects more feasible. By aligning interests and resources, you can create AI innovations greater than the sum of their parts, benefiting all stakeholders involved.

Negotiating effective collaboration agreements is crucial to the success of any partnership. Start by clearly defining roles and responsibilities for each partner. This clarity helps avoid misunderstandings and ensures that everyone knows what is expected of them. Addressing intellectual property (IP) sharing arrangements early on is equally important. Clearly outline how IP will be managed, whether jointly owned, licensed, or protected. This transparency fosters trust and minimizes potential conflicts down the line. Effective negotiation also involves open communication and flexibility. Be willing to adapt and compromise to meet the needs of all parties, creating a supportive environment where innovation can thrive. Once you have an explicit agreement, document it thoroughly to provide a reference point for future discussions and adjustments.

Leveraging partner networks can significantly enhance your reach and influence within the AI community. You gain access to a broader audience and valuable resources by tapping into your partners' networks. Cross-promotion opportunities with partners allow you to showcase your AI projects to new audiences, increasing visibility and potential adoption. This can include co-hosting events, sharing content, or jointly participating in industry conferences. Additionally, access to partner events and resources can provide unique learning and networking opportunities. Attend partner-hosted seminars, workshops, or meetings to expand your knowledge and connect with other experts in the field. By actively engaging with your partners' networks, you can build a robust presence in the AI community, fostering relationships that can lead to new collaborations and innovations.

11.3 HOSTING AI EVENTS: SHARING KNOWLEDGE AND INSPIRING ACTION

Imagine a room filled with the buzz of ideas and the clatter of keyboards as AI enthusiasts from diverse backgrounds gather to share their insights. Organizing such an event begins with setting clear objectives and themes. A successful AI conference should have a defined purpose: explore new trends, showcase innovations, or foster collaboration. Choosing a compelling theme helps attract the right audience and speakers. Consider what topics resonate in the AI community and how your event can address these interests. Once your theme is set, securing knowledgeable speakers and engaging panelists becomes essential. Reach out to industry leaders, researchers, and practitioners who can offer unique perspectives and spark meaningful discussions. Their insights enrich the event and draw attendees eager to learn from the best.

Engaging participants is the heart of any successful event, and interactive sessions are vital. Unlike traditional lectures, workshops and hands-on demos encourage active learning and participation. These sessions allow attendees to apply what they've learned, fostering a deeper understanding of the material. Consider including AI demos where participants can experiment with new technologies or tools. Such hands-on experiences make the concepts more tangible and memorable.

Additionally, Q&A sessions with AI experts allow attendees to ask questions and explore topics in greater depth. These interactions clarify complex ideas and create a dynamic learning environment where speakers and participants exchange knowledge freely. By incorporating interactive elements, your event becomes a platform for inspiration and education, leaving attendees with practical skills and valuable insights.

Creating networking opportunities during your event enhances its value by fostering participant connections. Designate areas for informal discussions where attendees can engage in spontaneous conversations. These spaces encourage networking mixers and breakout sessions, allowing individuals to exchange ideas and build relationships. Consider organizing structured networking activities, such as speed networking or roundtable discussions, to facilitate introductions and ensure that everyone has a chance to connect. These interactions can lead to collaborations, partnerships, or mentorship opportunities extending beyond the event. By providing a conducive environment for networking, you enable participants to expand their professional circles and explore new possibilities. These connections often become the backbone of future projects and innovations, reinforcing the event's impact long after it concludes.

After the event, evaluating its success is crucial for continuous improvement. Gathering feedback from attendees through post-event surveys and feedback forms provides insights into what worked well and what could be enhanced. Encourage honest and constructive feedback to comprehensively understand participants' experiences. Reviewing attendance and engagement metrics can offer additional data to assess the event's reach and impact. Analyze these metrics to identify trends and areas for growth, such as which sessions were most popular or where participants expressed the most interest. Use this information to refine future events, ensuring they meet the evolving needs of your audience. By continually evaluating and improving your events, you build a reputation for quality and relevance, attracting more participants and fostering a thriving AI community.

In essence, hosting AI events is a powerful way to bring people together, share knowledge, and inspire action. Each element, from planning to evaluation, plays a role in creating a memorable and impactful experience. As you engage with the community, you contribute to the collective knowledge and strengthen the bonds that drive the AI field forward.

CHAPTER 12

Resources and Tools for AI Success

Imagine sitting at your desk with a cup of coffee, staring at your computer screen filled with possibilities. You're about to embark on a journey to revolutionize your business using artificial intelligence. The world of AI offers a treasure trove of tools designed to elevate your entrepreneurial efforts to new heights. Whether you're looking to streamline operations, enhance customer interactions, or unlock new market insights, AI tools can be your compass. This chapter explores essential AI tools that cater to various business needs, ensuring you have the right resources at your fingertips to drive success.

Navigating the vast sea of AI software, it's crucial to identify tools that can genuinely make a difference. TensorFlow stands out as a must-have for those interested in machine learning. Developed by Google Brain, TensorFlow provides a robust platform for building and deploying machine learning models. Its flexibility and scalability make it ideal for entrepreneurs looking to integrate AI into their products and services. Another powerful tool is IBM Watson, renowned for its natural language processing capabilities. Watson can analyze text and speech, providing insights and transforming how businesses interact with customers. By harnessing these tools, you unlock the potential to innovate and improve efficiency across multiple business functions.

For those eager to delve deeper into AI development, platforms like Google Cloud AI Platform and Amazon SageMaker offer comprehensive environments to create and deploy AI applications. Google Cloud AI Platform provides tools that support every stage of machine learning, from data preparation to model training and deployment. Its seamless integration with other Google services ensures a smooth workflow, making it a favorite among developers. Similarly, Amazon SageMaker simplifies the process of building, training, and deploying machine learning models at scale. It offers a wide range of features, including built-in algorithms and support for multiple frameworks, enabling you to focus on innovation rather than infrastructure. These platforms provide the flexibility and power to bring your AI ideas to life.

For entrepreneurs needing deep technical expertise, user-friendly AI applications offer a gateway to harnessing AI'sbenefits without the steep learning curve. Rapid Miner is an excellent choice for data science workflows, offering an intuitive interface that simplifies complex processes. With Rapid Miner, you can analyze and visualize data, gaining valuable insights to inform your business decisions. MonkeyLearn, on the other hand, specializes in text analysis, allowing you to extract meaningful information from unstructured data like customer feedback and social media comments. Both tools prioritize usability, making them accessible to entrepreneurs who want to leverage AI without becoming data scientists.

Incorporating AI capabilities into existing systems is made effortless through APIs, which serve as bridges between your business applications and powerful AI functions. Google Vision API is beneficial for image recognition tasks, enabling you to analyze visual content and extract valuable data. Whether identifying objects in photos or analyzing brand sentiment in images, this API opens new avenues for understanding and engaging with your audience. Microsoft Azure Cognitive Services provides a suite of APIs that deliver AI-driven insights, from natural language understanding to speech recognition. These tools empower businesses to enhance their applications with advanced AI features, driving innovation and competitive advantage.

Resource List: Must-Have AI Tools for Entrepreneurs

1. **TensorFlow:** Ideal for machine learning development, offering scalability and flexibility.
2. **IBM Watson:** Excels in natural language processing, transforming customer interactions.
3. **Google Cloud AI Platform:** Comprehensive support for machine learning workflows.
4. **Amazon SageMaker:** Simplifies model training and deployment, focusing on innovation.
5. **RapidMiner:** User-friendly data science tool for accessible data analysis.
6. **MonkeyLearn:** Specializes in text analysis, extracting insights from unstructured data.
7. **Google Vision API:** Enables robust image recognition and analysis capabilities.
8. **Microsoft Azure Cognitive Services:** Delivers a range of AI-driven insights for business applications.

These AI tools are not just technological marvels but your allies in pursuing business excellence. As you explore their capabilities, consider how each can align with your strategic objectives, enhancing your ability to innovate and thrive in an increasingly digital world.

12.1 ONLINE COURSES AND CERTIFICATIONS: ENHANCING AI SKILLS

In today's fast-paced world, staying ahead means continually upgrading your skills, especially in fields as dynamic as artificial intelligence. Online courses provide a flexible way to gain these skills, allowing you to learn at your own pace and schedule. One standout course is "Machine Learning" by Andrew Ng on Coursera, which offers a comprehensive introduction to AI. This course covers everything from basic algorithms to advanced machine learning concepts, providing a solid foundation for anyone looking to integrate AI into their business strategies. Another excellent option is"AI for Everyone" by IBM on edX, designed to demystify AI for non-technical audiences. This course explains AI'spractical applications and explores how it can be leveraged in various industries, making it ideal for entrepreneurs eager to understand AI's potential.

Certifications can also significantly boost your credibility and expertise in the AI field. Stanford's AI Certificate Program is highly regarded, offering an in-depth exploration of AI's principles and applications. This program enhances your understanding of AI and adds a prestigious credential to your resume, distinguishing you as a knowledgeable professional in this competitive field. Similarly, the Professional Certificate in Machine Learning by edX provides a well-rounded education in machine learning, equipping you with the skills to apply AI technologies effectively in your business. These certifications validate your expertise and signal your commitment to staying at the forefront of technological innovation.

For those with specific interests or needs, specialized courses offer a deep dive into niche areas of AI. Udacity's "Deep Learning Nanodegree" is a prime example, focusing on neural networks and their applications. This course is particularly beneficial for entrepreneurs interested in harnessing the power of deep learning to solve complex business challenges. DataCamp's "Natural Language Processing with Python" is another specialized course that delves into the intricacies of NLP, offering insights into how this technology can be used to analyze and interpret human language. By enrolling in these courses, you can tailor your learning journey to align with your business's strategic goals, ensuring you acquire the skills most relevant to your industry.

Continuous learning remains vital as AI technology rapidly evolves. Platforms like Pluralsight offer AI learning paths that update you on the latest advancements and best practices. These paths allow you to explore various AI topics, from fundamental concepts to cutting-edge developments, ensuring you remain informed and agile in a constantly shifting landscape. LinkedIn Learning also provides many AI courses that cater to different skill levels and interests, enabling you to expand your knowledge base and stay competitive. These platforms facilitate ongoing education, helping you adapt to new technologies and integrate them seamlessly into your business operations.

Investing in your AI education enhances your capabilities and empowers you to make informed decisions that drive business growth. By leveraging the courses and certifications available, you can comprehensively understand AI's potential and how to apply it strategically. This knowledge positions you as a leader in your field and equips you with the tools to innovate, optimize, and thrive in an increasingly AI-driven world. As you explore these educational opportunities, consider how each course aligns with your personal and professional goals, ensuring your learning journey is both purposeful and impactful.

12.2 BOOKS AND PUBLICATIONS: STAYING INFORMED AND INSPIRED

Think about the transformative power of books, especially in AI, where knowledge is as vast as it is dynamic. Reading can be one of your most valuable tools in understanding and keeping pace with this rapidly evolving field. Consider"Artificial Intelligence: A Guide to Intelligent Systems" by Michael Negnevitsky. This book breaks down complex AI concepts into digestible insights, making it a fantastic starting point for anyone eager to understand intelligent systems'inner workings. It covers a broad spectrum of AI technologies and their practical applications, providing a solid foundation for further exploration. Another thought-provoking read is "Superintelligence: Paths, Dangers, Strategies" by Nick Bostrom. This book delves into the potential future of AI, exploring what might happen if machine intelligence surpasses human intelligence. Bostrom's work is crucial for entrepreneurs who wish to consider the ethical implications and strategic planning needed in an AI-driven future.

Industry journals and magazines are equally crucial in updating AI advancements and trends. The MIT Technology Review's AI section is a treasure trove of cutting-edge research and industry insights. It offers articles ranging from technical deep dives to broader analyses of how AI reshapes industries worldwide. Keeping this publication within reach can ensure you're always informed about the latest breakthroughs and innovations. Similarly, the Journal of Artificial Intelligence Research is an essential resource for those looking to understand the nitty-gritty details of AI research. It presents scholarly articles that delve into AI's technical challenges and advancements, offering a more profound understanding that can inform strategic business decisions. Regularly engaging with these publications can significantly enhance your knowledge and keep you ahead in the competitive AI landscape.

Inspirational narratives can also serve as a catalyst for creativity and innovation. "The Master Algorithm" by Pedro Domingos is one such book examining the quest for a universal algorithm capable of learning anything. Domingos presents a fascinating exploration of machine learning's potential, sparking ideas on how such concepts could be applied to various business contexts. Stuart Russell's "Human Compatible: Artificial Intelligence and the Problem of Control" is another must-read. It addresses the profound challenges of aligning advanced AI systems with human values, a critical consideration for entrepreneurs looking to implement AI ethically and responsibly. These narratives do more than inform; they inspire and challenge you to think differently about AI's role in the world and your business.

Online, a wealth of information is available through blogs and websites dedicated to AI. The Towards Data Science blog is an excellent resource for actionable insights and tutorials on data science and AI. It offers a platform for practitioners to share lessons learned and innovative techniques, making it a valuable community for ongoing learning and inspiration. OpenAI's official blog is another noteworthy source, providing updates on new AI models and research findings directly from one of the field's leading organizations. Engaging with these online resources can offer fresh perspectives and keep you connected to a community of like-minded individuals equally passionate about AI.

Reflection Section: Your Personal AI Reading List

Consider creating a personal reading list that includes the books and publications mentioned here. Reflect on how each resource aligns with your business goals and personal interests. This list can serve as a roadmap for your ongoing education in AI, ensuring you stay informed and inspired as you navigate the opportunities and challenges of integrating AI into your entrepreneurial journey.

12.3 SUPPORT NETWORKS: FINDING MENTORS AND ADVISORS IN AI

Imagine standing at the crossroads of AI integration, excited and overwhelmed by the possibilities. What you need at this moment is guidance from those who've walked this path before. AI mentorship programs serve as invaluable resources, connecting you with seasoned experts who can illuminate your journey. Programs like AI for Good's mentorship initiatives are designed to foster connections between entrepreneurs and experienced AI practitioners. These initiatives offer personalized guidance and provide a platform for exchanging ideas and solving complex problems. Similarly, the Global AI Talent Accelerator focuses on nurturing talent by pairing entrepreneurs with mentors who can offer strategic insights and practical advice. Engaging in these programs allows you to tap into a wealth of knowledge, ensuring you're equipped to confidently navigate the fast-paced world of AI.

Being part of AI-focused networking groups can open doors you never knew existed. These groups provide fertile ground for collaboration, innovation, and learning. Attending AI meetups and conferences immerses you in an environment where ideas flow freely and connections are forged. These gatherings attract a diverse array of professionals, from developers and data scientists to business leaders, each bringing unique perspectives to the table. Like Reddit's Machine Learning subreddit, online forums extend these interactions into the digital realm, offering a space for ongoing dialogue and support. These communities are invaluable for staying updated on the latest developments, discussing challenges, and finding inspiration in others' successes. By actively participating in these spaces, you position yourself at the heart of the AI community, ready to seize opportunities as they arise.

Advisory boards are another crucial component of a robust support network. These boards consist of industry experts who provide strategic guidance on AI implementation, ensuring your projects align with industry standards and best practices. Industry-specific AI advisory panels offer insights tailored to your sector, helping you navigate your field's unique challenges and opportunities. Meanwhile, university-affiliated AI advisory groups bring together academics and practitioners, creating a rich exchange of ideas and fostering innovation. Engaging with these boards allows you to better understand AI's potential applications and risks, equipping you with the knowledge needed to make informed decisions. These relationships enhance your strategic planning and build a reputation for thought leadership within your industry.

In today's interconnected world, online mentorship platforms are revolutionizing how we connect with experts. Platforms like MentorCruise facilitate connections between entrepreneurs and AI professionals, offering a flexible and accessible way to seek advice and mentorship. These platforms allow you to browse mentors based on expertise, experience, and availability, ensuring you find the right fit for your needs. Additionally, Meetup provides a valuable resource for finding local AI mentors who can offer guidance and support in person. These platforms democratize access to mentorship, breaking down geographical barriers and enabling you to learn from the best, regardless of location. By leveraging these tools, you can build a network of trusted advisors supporting your growth and success in AI.

As we conclude this chapter, remember that building a support network is not just about seeking help but about creating opportunities for collaboration and growth. By connecting with mentors, joining networking groups, engaging with advisory boards, and utilizing online platforms, you empower yourself to navigate the complexities of AI with confidence and clarity. This network becomes a vital resource, providing the insights and support needed to thrive in this dynamic field. Keep these connections at hand as you continue your exploration into AI, knowing they are there to guide you toward success.

Conclusion

As you reach the end of this journey, remember that embracing artificial intelligence can transform your entrepreneurial endeavors. This book was crafted with the central message that AI is not just a tool but a gateway to discovering new avenues for building wealth. By integrating AI into your business, you unlock a world of opportunities where efficiency, innovation, and profitability converge.

These chapters have explored how AI can enhance various business facets, from streamlining operations to improving customer experiences. We've delved into its transformative power across retail, healthcare, finance, and manufacturing industries. Each chapter has been a stepping stone, offering actionable insights and practical strategies to apply to your unique business context.

Chapter by chapter, we began by demystifying AI, breaking down its components and capabilities. We then moved into the heart of AI's role in business, illustrating how it drives efficiency and boosts profitability with real-world examples. We've discussed the economics of AI, showing how it offers cost-effective solutions that can scale with your business. The myths surrounding AI were debunked, assuring you that it's not just for tech giants. Small companies, too, can thrive by integrating AI into their strategies.

As you consider the value of AI integration, remember that it's not merely about keeping up with trends. It's about gaining a competitive edge, leveraging technology to cut costs and drive innovation. Whether automating customer service, optimizing your supply chain, or personalizing marketing efforts, AI opens doors to new efficiencies and revenue streams.

We also addressed the challenges you might face as you embark on this journey. Integrating AI into your business has challenges, from technical hurdles to skill gaps. But with practical solutions and a step-by-step roadmap, you're equipped to overcome these barriers. By starting small, leveraging accessible tools, and investing in learning, you can gradually scale your AI capabilities.

Now, it's time for action. Please take the first steps to leverage AI for your ventures. Explore the tools, invest in learning, and engage with the vibrant AI community. The world of AI is ever-evolving, and staying updated with advancements is critical to refining your strategies.

Fostering a community mindset is equally crucial. Connect with other AI-driven entrepreneurs, share your knowledge, and learn from their experiences. Together, you can promote a supportive and innovative community that thrives on collaboration and shared success.

As I close, I want to reiterate my passion for helping entrepreneurs like you overcome financial barriers and succeed through AI. This book has provided you with valuable guidance and inspiration. Your journey is just beginning, and I look forward to seeing how you harness AI to transform your business.

Finally, I invite you to share your experiences, feedback, and success stories. Feel free to reach out with questions or insights. Let's keep this dialogue going and continue to learn and grow together in this exciting AI-driven world.

References

11 AI Tools for Small Businesses (Low Cost, Big Impact!) https://www.dialpad.com/blog/ai-tools-for-small-business/

AI in Business: Enhancing Efficiency and Reducing Costs https://indatalabs.com/blog/ai-cost-reduction

Evolution of Artificial Intelligence in Business https://litslink.com/blog/evolution-artificial-intelligence-in-business

Debunking AI Myths for Small Business Success https://businessnucleus.com/common-myths-and-misconceptions-about-ai/

How Small Businesses Are Using AI—And How Yours Can ...https://www.forbes.com/sites/allbusiness/2023/11/17/how-small-businesses-are-using-ai-and-how-your-business-can-benefit-too/

Data Governance Best Practices for 2024 Success https://atlan.com/data-governance-best-practices/

65 Artificial Intelligence (AI) Companies to Know https://builtin.com/artificial-intelligence/ai-companies-roundup

The Complete No-Code AI Guide (Updated January 2024) https://www.akkio.com/post/no-code-ai-tools-complete-guide

*Customer Service: How AI Is Transforming Interactions - Forbes*https://www.forbes.com/councils/forbesbusinesscouncil/2024/08/22/customer-service-how-ai-is-transforming-interactions/

Benefits of AI in Supply Chain - Oracle https://www.oracle.com/scm/ai-supply-chain/

Predictive Analytics in Marketing: 7 Use Cases https://www.itransition.com/predictive-analytics/marketing

How generative AI can help banks manage risk and ... https://www.mckinsey.com/capabilities/risk-and-resilience/our-insights/how-generative-ai-can-help-banks-manage-risk-and-compliance

Better, Faster, Cheaper, Safer: Why AI must replace human ... https://medium.com/@dave-shap/better-faster-cheaper-safer-why-ai-must-replace-human-labor-20203020f5f7

Small Businesses And Their CEOS Are Starting To Find ...https://www.forbes.com/sites/zengernews/2023/08/26/small-businesses-and-their-ceos-are-starting-to-find-success-with-ai/

9 AI Use Cases in Major Industries | 2024 Guide https://acropolium.com/blog/ai-use-cases-in-major-industries-elevate-your-business-with-disruptive-technology/

11 Challenges of AI Startups & How to Address Them https://www.oracle.com/artifi cial-intelligence/ai-startup-challenges/

Comparing the Cost of Generative AI vs. IVR vs. Human ... https://waterfieldtech. com/insights/the-cost-of-generative-ai-vs-ivr-vs-human/

10 Essential Steps for Successfully Implementing AI in ... https://www.journeyteam. com/resources/blog/10-essential-steps-for-successfully-implementing-ai-in-your- business/

Proven open source AI technology and tools in 2023 https://codingscape.com/blog/ proven-open-source-ai-technology-and-tools-in-2023

11 Advantages of Cloud-Based AI: Gain an Edge to ... https://www.tierpoint.com/ blog/advantages-of-cloud-based-ai/

How to Calculate AI ROI for Your Business https://www.multimodal.dev/post/how- to-calculate-ai-roi

12 Benefits of Real-Time Analytics for Businesses - Oracle https://www.oracle.com/ mysql/real-time-analytics-benefits/

Comparing the Cost of Generative AI vs. IVR vs. Human ... https://waterfieldtech. com/insights/the-cost-of-generative-ai-vs-ivr-vs-human/

How businesses can measure AI success with KPIs https://www.techtarget.com/ searchenterpriseai/tip/How-businesses-can-measure-AI-success-with-KPIs

Ethics of Artificial Intelligence | UNESCO https://www.unesco.org/en/artificial-intel ligence/recommendation-ethics

GDPR vs CCPA: A thorough breakdown of data protection ... https://thoropass.com/ blog/compliance/gdpr-vs-ccpa/

AI Risk Management Framework https://www.nist.gov/itl/ai-risk-management-frame work

Building Trust In AI: The Case For Transparency https://www.forbes.com/sites/ bernardmarr/2024/05/03/building-trust-in-ai-the-case-for-transparency/

*How AI-Powered Personalization Is Reshaping Online ...*https://www.forbes.com/ councils/forbestechcouncil/2023/10/16/how-ai-powered-personalization-is- reshaping-online-shopping-and-beyond/

How AI Is Improving Diagnostics, Decision-Making and Care https://www.aha.org/ aha-center-health-innovation-market-scan/2023-05-09-how-ai-improving-diag nostics-decision-making-and-care

AI-Powered Financial Fraud Detection in Banking https://www.infosysbpm.com/ blogs/bpm-analytics/fraud-detection-with-ai-in-banking-sector.html

*Artificial Intelligence In Manufacturing: Four Use Cases ...*https://www.forbes.com/ sites/bernardmarr/2023/07/07/artificial-intelligence-in-manufacturing-four-use- cases-you-need-to-know-in-2023/

*Quantum Artificial Intelligence Is Closer Than You Think*https://www.forbes.com/

sites/jonathanreichental/2023/11/20/quantum-artificial-intelligence-is-closer-than-you-think/

How Edge AI is Powering the Future of Smart Cities? https://www.xenonstack.com/blog/edge-ai-future-smart-cities#:~

How Does AI Drive Autonomous Systems? https://scienceexchange.caltech.edu/topics/artificial-intelligence-research/autonomous-ai-cars-drones

What is AI Governance? https://www.ibm.com/topics/ai-governance

How Leaders Can Build an AI-Ready Culture https://www.innosight.com/insight/build-an-ai-ready-culture/

AI Leadership: Why AI Is Every Leader's Responsibility https://www.forbes.com/sites/sherzododilov/2024/07/14/ai-leadership-why-ai-is-every-leaders-responsibility/

AI Adoption Strategy: Maximizing AI Tool Usage | Moveworks https://www.moveworks.com/us/en/resources/blog/ai-adoption-strategy-for-a-successful-ai-integration#:~

AI success factor: Cross-functional teams - Insights2Action https://action.deloitte.com/insight/3236/ai-success-factor-cross-functional-teams#:~

10 AI Conferences You Need to Attend in 2024 https://www.vfairs.com/blog/ai-conferences/

The Best AI Communities Online https://aiproducthive.com/index.php/2024/05/27/the-best-ai-communities-online/

AI Startups in the Era of Big Tech: Fostering Mutually ... https://www.magnetmediafilms.com/story/ai-startups-in-the-era-of-big-tech-fostering-mutually-beneficial-partnerships-and-innovation

AI Tools for Event Planners: The Complete Guide https://www.bizzabo.com/guides/complete-ai-guide-for-event-planners

The 8 Best AI Tools for Entrepreneurs & Startups in 2024 https://altar.io/the-best-ai-tools-for-entrepreneurs-startups/

10 Top Artificial Intelligence Certifications And Courses For ... https://www.techtarget.com/whatis/feature/10-top-artificial-intelligence-certifications-and-courses

11 Books on Artificial Intelligence That Will Make You Think https://qat.com/11-books-artificial-intelligence/

AI-Powered Mentorship Programs - Hyperspace https://hyperspace.mv/ai-mentorship/#:~

www.ingramcontent.com/pod-product-compliance
Lightning Source LLC
Chambersburg PA
CBHW071512220526
45472CB00003B/1000